Communi

How to Increase Your

Reading Speed

The dear people
do not know
how long it takes
to learn to read.
I have been at it
all my life
and I cannot yet say
I have reached the goal.

GOETHE

Communication Skills

How to Increase Your Reading Speed

An invaluable guide to the art of rapid reading

Pramila Ahuja
and
G. C. Ahuja

A Sterling Paperback

STERLING PAPERBACKS
An imprint of
Sterling Publishers (P) Ltd.
A-59, Okhla Industrial Area, Phase-II,
New Delhi-110020.
Tel: 26387070, 26386209; Fax: 91-11-26383788
E-mail: sterlingpublishers@airtelbroadband.in
ghai@nde.vsnl.net.in
www.sterlingpublishers.com

How to Increase Your Reading Speed

ISBN 81 207 1797 X

Printed and Published by
Sterling Publishers Pvt. Ltd., New Delhi-110 020.

PREFACE

The dependence of man upon interchange of thoughts and opinions through the medium of printed lines is immeasurable. To imagine a day without reading is impossible. Reading enters into nearly every phase of life. It has unique contributions to make. Reading is an avenue of learning—a tool, a means to an end. Initially, we learn to read, but thereafter we read to learn. Reading is important for the leisure of life, no less than for the work of life. It contributes to personal as well as to professional growth. It helps to make the life richer and more meaningful. Reading is a form of experience through which horizons may be expanded and this leads to personality development.

Many students at collegiate and university level, and adults engaged in a variety of undertakings are much slower readers than they need to be. They read everything so slowly as if all the time they were reading legal documents.

We are living in a fast moving world. We have been able to speed up practically everything to fit the modern tempo—communication, transportation, calculation and what not! But even today, we are where we were, as far as reading speed is concerned.

There was a time when we were not having plenty of reading materials, hence nobody thought of reading speed. We thus used to read leisurely and developed habitually slow reading habits. Each one of us has the capacity to read much faster but we never made use of it. At the present moment we are finding ourselves amidst a great knowledge explosion. There is so much to read today that the ability to read rapidly has become an important asset.

Almost all the professions require much reading during the period of preparation, as well as continued reading while being in the profession if one is to keep pace with the new developments.

Rapid reading habits enable a person to get more in a comparatively lesser time which is the demand of the hour. We are living a very busy life and hardly find any time to keep ourselves fully informed with what is going on around us. The possession of rapid reading ability comes to our rescue in our busy schedule. It helps us in enriching our life with plenty of reading materials undertaking and rendering greater service to the mankind.

The purpose of this book is to acquaint the readers with the different procedures and practices of increasing reading rates. The book deals with the complexities of the reading process which is the very basis of reading speed. With little effort and systematic practice one can become a better, economical, efficient and versatile reader able to cope more competently with the present day reading demands.

The authors owe a sense of gratitude to many scholars in the field whose contributions have inspired them. Special appreciation and acknowledgements are due to all the reading specialists from whose works the authors have liberally drawn.

The content of this book reflects both our experiences and commitment for conducting Rapid Reading courses. In particular, the book could not have been written had we not been influenced —rather indoctrinated, by the academic atmosphere of the Central Institute of Indian Languages, Mysore, of which Dr D. P. Pattanayak, is the Director. Our sincere thanks are due to him. It is needless to mention that the views expressed in the book are our own and do not necessarily reflect the policies of the Institute.

A final word: This book will not only prove to be useful for readers in every field but also for secondary school teachers, university students, lecturers, research workers, and above all those who want to understand the mechanics and methods of efficient reading. For those who are interested in speeding up their reading, this book has a great message to give.

Pramila Ahuja
G. C. Ahuja

CONTENTS

1

UNDERSTANDING THE NATURE OF READING

Ours is a reading world. A child reads, an adolescent reads, an adult reads and even an old man enjoys reading. People read in the morning, they read during lunch hour and they read even after a day's hard work. Some are in the habit of reading a lot before going to sleep. They even report that they need some type of reading before they go to bed, otherwise they do not enjoy a sound sleep. Many people are not able to digest their food unless they read some thing immediately after a meal. In the present-day busy life it is not very uncommon to find people devoting each and every spare moment to reading.

Today we are engulfed by plenty of reading materials. Modern men read to be informed, entertained, enlightened, stimulated and comforted. In this Jet age, it has become all the more important to process a big bulk of information of wide variety through reading, and to process it with a reasonable degree of speed and a high degree of accuracy. One can hardly dispute the fact that reading has many uses.

Reading affects the entire personality of an individual. The readers become totally new 'being' after they had read something which is really of value to them.

In *What Reading Does to People,* Waples[1] reports the results of his studies of the effects of reading on groups of people. He has identified five general areas:

(*a*) The instrumental effect: the results of reading for knowledge, information.

(*b*) The prestige effect: the results of reading for self-approval.

(*c*) The aesthetic effect: the results of reading for the beauty of expression.

(*d*) The respite effect: the results of reading that relieves tension.

(*e*) The reinforcement effect: the results of reading that reaffirms our attitudes.

Why Read at All

Good literature has no dimensions or limitations, and readers or listeners are free to take from it what they will. A good book gives you a life you haven't had the time to live and it gives you a geography, an imaginative landscape you cannot enter physically. A great book is different from a good book in the size of the landscape and in the dimension of the light it gives you. If you think you can get to be a full human being without having any contact with the experiences stored in the good and great books of the world I think you are wrong. It need not be any one list. I am talking about reading not as a matter of accumulating facts, that's a separate and an entirely respectable process, but as a process of accumulating experiences.[2]

Mark Van Doren,[3] from his eminent position in the field of literature, has this to say about reading:

"Every book that is worth reading is one that makes us want to read the next page no matter what it is ... We're always reading in the expectation of what will come next ... We have done the thing that reading demands—we have sat down alone and silent to give our minds to another, to surrender ourselves to somebody else who has written this thing. The reader is a surrenderer first and last ... I believe studies have been made, psychological tests, of persons reading. It is an active experience. No one reads perfectly relaxed. No one reads as if he were just sort of letting something pass him by. Anyone who is truly reading is grasping, seizing something and working with it ... The desire to read is the desire to know. We read because we want to know more. And of course I mean more than the desire for information. It finally means, when it's most exciting and interesting, the desire to know what we already know and yet do not know that we do ... I personally believe that every student should be asked at least once a day to read out something loud and make sense of it, real sense. Until he has learned to do that, and I mean something that he never saw before, I believe he is not a reader. The way he can prove to you that he is a reader is when he can read something aloud so that he can understand it and furthermore like it ... I think we should reveal that reading is an art and what is read is a form of art because writing is an art ... The sentence is the heartbeat of the mind ... All there is to reading after all is reading a book one sentence at a time—not one word at a time, but one sentence at a time—not missing any sentence and not missing what is there."

Lawrence E. Hafner[4] does not deny the unique values of modern communication media such as radio and television in education circles but according to his view compared with such forms of communication media, reading has the following values:

1. Reading material is readily accessible.
2. Reader can react as an individual.
3. Reading allows time for reflection.
4. Information is easily rechecked.
5. Memories can be renewed.
6. One can select segments of material he wants.
7. Sources can be compared readily.
8. One can readily skim a wide range of material.
9. One can check on the credentials of the author.
10. Reading provides excellent contexts for concept development and vocabulary study.

Reading is a tool. It is a means to an end. Who does not like to read? Even children who are not able to decode the printed symbols like to read and they do read. They just take the book or magazine and take pride in turning the pages and moving their lips simultaneously to prove that they are reading. Their lip movements with typical sounds—what they mean they only know; but if you just ask a child what you are doing—he will give you a spontaneous answer—'I am reading'. 'Yah—I know how to read.' Everybody, may he be a child or a grown-up, appears to read in his own typical, unique, and different style. They all want to reach the same destination through the medium of reading. A well read person is respected everywhere. We can never underestimate the returns which this tool gives us throughout our lives. The person who has a thorough mastery in the use of this tool is really a privileged person. In a democracy like India, reading always holds a high position. It is important that people be skilled readers not only in their ability to understand the printed page but also in their ability and disposition to evaluate what they have read. Skilful reading demands thinking. Different occasions require us to read for different purposes. We read for pleasure, we read for specific information, we read to locate material dealing with special problems and many a time we read aloud to share information with others. When there is so much importance of this tool, we are bound to ask ourselves—what is reading? What skills does it involve? Is it a simple process or a complex process? Is it a natural phenomenon or does one labour hard for acquiring it? Let us ponder over the issue and try to find out the answers to some of the questions posed above.

Reading: What It Is

Johns[5] studied the views of junior schoolers on reading and listed the following as the representative ones:

1. Reading is a book. If you do not know the words, sound them out.
2. Reading is when you see a group of words in a sentence.
3. We read stories and do workbook pages.
4. Reading is something you do to learn from books.

5. Reading is something you do when you look at the words and you say them aloud or silently.
6. Reading is when you read a word and it tells you something.
7. You see, words have names and they have certain letters. You look at the letters and you put them together and you read a whole bunch of words together.
8. Reading is when you say a bunch of words.

In a parallel study[6] where the pupils of classes V to VII were involved, the following representative views were gathered.

1. Reading is the thing what we read every day in our schools.
2. Reading means to learn something.
3. Reading means what we read.
4. Reading is to read with our mouth.
5. Reading means we can read some stories.
6. Reading is reading.
7. Reading means to read in mind.
8. Reading means to take a book and pronounce the words.

The high school teachers engaged in teaching languages in different parts of our country, when asked 'what is reading?' gave various interpretations. Some of the representative ones have been reproduced below.[7]

1. Reading is the ability of the vocal cords to pronounce correctly the written materials.
2. Reading is an expression of sentences in correct forms.
3. Reading is the media of expressing words and sentences in correct intonation.
4. Reading means silent and loud reading.
5. Reading is a fine art of speech.

It is very clear that everybody seems to have a vague idea of the reading process but nobody knows the delicacies of this complex activity.

Understanding Reading

Reading is both a sensory and a mental process. It involves use of the eye and the mind. Reduced to word calling—which is not reading, it becomes only a sensorial activity which only takes into account the work of the eye without taking into consideration the brain mechanism. Reading is a visual and mental phenomenon.[8]

Betts[9] is of the opinion that reading is a process rather than a subject. The development of efficient and versatile habits of reading and study is a continuous process which cannot be terminated when the pupil is admitted to the intermediate grades or to the secondary school. Since reading is primarily a thinking process, reading ability cannot be fully developed in the primary school. If this viewpoint is translated into practice, then very definite provision for systematic guidance in reading should be made in the secondary school. Furthermore, the fact that one does not read "reading" but reads literature, science, social studies, mathematics, and the like, places the responsibility for systematic instruction on all teachers. In short, systematic instruction for the development of efficient reading habits is the responsibility of every teacher.

Gray[10] in his identification of the three so-called definitions of reading describes: 'one of these definitions limits reading to the interpretation of written and printed symbols; a second assumes that reading includes the interpretation of all symbols or signs which denote or represent or stand for something else; a third conceives reading as the process of making intellectual adjustments to stimuli from various sources including natural signs as well as conventional symbols.'

To Artley,[11] real reading means plucking out all the subtle threads of meaning from sentences, paragraphs, and pages and weaving them into your own personality.

The modern point of view sees reading not as a group of skills but as a part of the well-rounded development of children and adults. The "complete" reader is the individual who not only has mastered the mechanics of reading but who is interested in pursuing ideas or recreation through more and more reading, who brings back nuggets from his reading to the rest of the group, who weighs and appraises as he reads. The complete reading act, similarly, is not limited to perception and interpretation of symbols; it is perception plus understanding plus interpretation plus use. The reading act is complete only when judgement enters and when the earlier steps are put to work in such forms as ideas retained for future use, notes recorded for a talk or plans made for a later activity.[12]

Levels of Reading Comprehension

Gray[13] suggested that different levels of meaning could be obtained from the same material. He identified a literal level, which involves translation of what the words say, an interpretative level, which relates material to its context, a significance level, which involves implications, and an evaluative level, which requires the reader to react to the material in his own terms. Robinson[14] developed a model in which the different aspects of reading interacted, depending on the ability of the reader and his purpose. The four quadrants of her model are word perception, comprehension, reaction and assimilation. Involved with all these parts is the rate of reading, which influences the excellence of the reading patterns on any dimension. Robinson describes word perception as both word recognition and word meaning; comprehension includes literal and implied meanings; reaction involves intellectual judgements and emotional responses. She does not subdivide assimilation.

Clymer[15] provided an illustration of the relationship between the complexity of reading outcomes and the linguist's definition of what is called reading. The most basic level is decoding, which is conceded by all authorities to be a part of reading. The second level, grasping the author's meaning which is similar to literal translation in Gray's classification, is a step more complex and, therefore, excluded by some linguists from the domain of reading. Clymer's third level of complexity involves testing and combining the author's messages. This is a higher order of comprehension than literal translation and is excluded from the definition of reading by an increased number of linguists. Application and extension, which are similar to Robinson's assimilation, are at the top of the complexity sequence. Most linguists exclude application activities from their definition of reading.

Decoding Is Not Enough

Recently a prominent linguist[16] wrote: Reading is the identification of linguistic forms from strings of written configurations that represent them, as evidenced by producing the conventional signs for the 'same, linguistic forms in some other system of representation ... Any one who has learned to read can read many sentences whose meanings are almost completely unknown to him'.

A University Professor of Romance language makes the following comparison:[17] Reading involves the responding to visual forms with vocal or sub-vocal ones. The "thoughtful" or "meaningful" reactions that accompany or follow this process are responses to the vocalised or sub-vocalised forms and the underlying neurophysiology. Thus, while the reading specialist is inclined to say that "the printed word merely acts as a trigger that releases a meaning we already possess", the linguist believes that the printed word acts as a trigger that releases its oral counterpart, which, in its turn, releases a meaning we already possess.

The view has been forwarded that reading is simply the recognition or identification of the words represented by the printed symbols, regardless of whether or not meaning is achieved. Once a lady surprised a speaker of Marathi by reading aloud from a Marathi story book. "Oh, you know Marathi?" he asked. "No, I don't understand a word of it," she answered. "I can only read it."

A psycholinguist calls reading a psycholinguistic guessing game. On the basis of detailed analysis of fairly typical oral reading errors, Goodman[18] offered the following definition: "Reading is a selective process. It involves partial use of available minimum language cues selected from perceptual input on the basis of the reader's expectation. As the partial information is processed, tentative decisions are made to be confirmed, rejected or refined as reading progresses." This statement, when compared to Reed's, indicates how far linguists and psycholinguists are from agreement among themselves. Goodman's analysis corresponds closely to the viewpoint of most reading specialists.

Wiener and Cromer[19] have suggested that identification and comprehension have different significance in the acquisition and accomplished stages of reading. However, they go beyond, stating that identification is highly important in early reading, which is correct, and propose that "identification may be a necessary antecedent to comprehension".

The Complexity of Reading

Harris[20] is of the opinion that reading is a very complex process in which the recognition and comprehension of written symbols are influenced by the perceptual skills, the word analysis skills, the experience, the language background, the mindset and the reading ability of the readers, as they anticipate meaning on the basis of what they have just read. The total process is a *gestalt* or a whole in which a serious flaw in any major function or part may prevent adequate information.

To Russell,[21] reading is a subtle and complex act which involves more or less simultaneously, the following: sensation of light rays on the retina of the eye reaching the brain, perception of separate words and phrases, functioning of the eye muscles with exact controls, immediate memory for what has just been read, remote memories based on the reader's experience, interest in the context read, and organisation of the material so that finally it can be used in some way. These various features operate more or less concurrently; but they can be analysed into at least four successive stages: sensation, perception, comprehension and utilisation.

Professor Douglas Waples,[22] who has made many fine contributions to the sociology of reading, contributes to this notion: "Reading clarifies, formulates, and hence helps to express ideas born of the reader's common experience. The social effects of reading can be understood only in the social context which explains the community's hopes and fears. In short, reading is a social process. It relates the reader to his environment, and it conditions that relationship. To some aspects of the environment, the reader has a primary relationship; that is, he is in direct physical contact with them.

To other aspects of the environment, he holds a secondary relationship; he establishes contact only through symbols. Both sets of relationship make up his experience. Through reading, the individual may extend his secondary relationships with the environment; and they may do as much to condition him to make him what he is, as do his primary relationships. The extension of popular education, the improvements of communication methods, and the rapid increase in the scope of public communications are certain to increase the importance of such symbolic experience. In this context, reading is one channel among many through which the environment affects the individual ..."

Discussing about the nature of reading, Horn[23] presents very challenging and thought-provoking views: There is some disagreement as to how broadly reading should be defined. The mere recognition of words leading at times to their memorisation, although it involves some degree of reading ability, obviously stops at too low a level. Some writers prefer to limit the use of the term to understanding, varying from little to much, which accompanies the movement of the eyes along the lines of the printed page. Others would include also the selection, appraisal, reflection, and problem-solving that may be required for an adequate understanding of what is read. Still others would include under the term most of the processes associated with, and necessary to the effective use of books.

Reading is the deepening of perception and understanding through the intercommunication of minds using the medium of the written word. Reading is much more than mere word, phrase, or even sentence recognition. Reading involves not only the skills of word recognition (such as the use of configuration, contextual clues, and word analysis, which includes phonics as one of the basic means of word attack) but also comprehension, library, work-study, and appreciation skills. Reading includes the development of attitudes, abilities and techniques whose interrelationships are many, varied, and intricate. Reading has dimensions that go far above and beyond the literal meaning of the printed word. Reading concerns the context in which words expand into ideas and thoughts derived from past experiences. It involves the imagination, the thinking, and the feeling of both participants in the communicative process—the writer and the reader. Reading is a highly complex process, an expression of the total personality of the individual, and a vital facet of the language arts rather than a separate and discrete curriculum area.[24]

Reconstruction of the Facts behind the Symbols

Recently, Count Korzybsrki, the general semanticist, described reading as "the reconstruction of the facts behind the symbols". This notion of reading shifts the emphasis from the mechanics of reading to interpretation, in the larger sense, as the crux of communication.

Reading is sometimes referred to as mental constructs. Symbols do not contain any meanings in themselves—these work as partial stimulus for the reader. Comprehension is the product of reconstructing the facts within the nervous system of the reader.

Betts[25] is of the opinion that reading requires a "taking to" as well as a "taking from" a language situation. One man may look at the picture of an aeroplane and "see" only a streamlined machine that flies through the air. An engineer may look at the same picture and "see" examples of recognition or violations of fundamental principles of aerodynamics. In like manner, two individuals looking at the pen scratches or printed symbols on this page are not likely to "see" or "read" the same meanings into them. This fact of "taking to" reading situation is commented upon by Louis C. Zahner.[26]

... One of the cardinal principles of language is that words derive their meanings from their intricate connections with the world, the world of things and of men, in other words, from man's total experience in his environment of animate and inanimate creation. This is the foundation of the meaning of words.

Perhaps an all-inclusive definition of reading might be stated as follows:[27] Reading is recognising and interpreting symbolic language and interacting with it. This interaction may be any degree of acceptance or rejection of what is stated; enjoyment of the language itself; retention of fact, feeling or inspiration; stimulation to create; or any number of other positive or negative reactions. One never knows for sure what may result from the act of reading. Indirect influences may be felt far into the future.

In a broad view, reading is regarded as a manifold process that involves associating words with meanings and letter sounds with the printed symbols, thinking, feeling, acting, and becoming. Creative and thoughtful reading begins when the reader has learned how to find out what the author actually says.[28]

Decoding to Fluent Reading—A Continuum

As Smith[29] stated so forcibly in *Understanding Reading,* a clearer understanding of what the skilled reader can do, and of what the beginning reader is trying to do, is far more important for the teacher than any revision of instructional materials.

The 'decoding' that the skilled reader performs is not to transform visual symbols into sound, which is the widely held conventional view of what reading is about, but to transform the visual representation of languages into meaning.

The child, when he starts to read, does not require to be taught language but the written representation of language. He does not have to be taught to look; he has to be taught the significant characteristics of print. He needs to know enough, not all, about the letter. Fluent reading does not necessitate a minute analysis of each letter or word but only sufficient to extract meaning from the printed page. A large number of interrelated skills developed over a period of years are necessary for reading. Ability to recall nonsense syllables does not differentiate good and poor readers. 'If, to quote Merritt[30] the ability to anticipate sequences is the basis of fluent reading' then a willingness to make mistakes is likely to be part of the process of learning to read. 'Guessing' is only bad for a child if it is based on wrong cues. It may be, however, a stage in development of linguistic competence leading to fluent reading. The child has to discover the distinctive features of print, of words and of letters, and the teacher must, in order to assist in this development, provide not only examples, but contrasts.

To Betts[31], reading is an evaluational process which requires specialised types of integrated action. In other words, it is purposeful experiencing in which mechanics are subordinated to meaning.

Reading, therefore, is more than the reciprocative action of the eyes as they move discontinuously over each line of type; it is more than the ability demanded for mere word pronouncing; and it involves emotional patterns more intricate than those required for aimless and colourless oral reading to the teacher. In psychological terms, reading as a thinking process calls for purposeful interpretation, carrying a sequence of ideas in mind, association of immediate experience with a background of information and feelings, anticipation of meaning, organisation of ideas, drawing of inferences (or reading between the lines), use of judgement, and similar mental and emotional responses, depending upon the purpose of the reading and the type of material. Integrated with these psychological processes are certain patterns of seeing which vary with the demands of the reading task. In addition to reorientations of mental functions required by changes in the purpose of the reading (such as skimming, reading for general impression, reading for details), different visual patterns are brought into action. In the true sense of the word, therefore, reading is a dynamic rather than a static process, requiring constant changes in or reintegration of patterns of behaviour.

Moreover, if reading abilities, skills and attitudes are to be serviceable to the end of promoting efficient reading, then thought or meaning must be kept uppermost and the mechanics of the process must be reduced to automation.

In his book, *The Art of Loving,* Erich Fromm explains that there are different kinds of love and that these different kinds of love can be defined in a number of ways. The theory of love effects the practice of love: one's definition of love affects his general attitude towards love, the way he loves, whom he loves, and for what purposes he loves. In a similar way a person's definition of the reading process affects his attitude towards reading: the way he reads, what he will read, and for what purposes he will read.

Should we not then try to know about the reading process and even the science of reading for that matter? Let's now go to the next chapter which deals with the 'Science of Reading'.

SUMMARY

Reading is both a sensory and a mental process. It involves use of the eye and the mind. Reduced to word-calling—which is not reading, it becomes a sensorial activity which only takes into account the work of the eye without taking into consideration the brain mechanism. Reading is a visual and a mental phenomenon. Reading is a decoding and meaning-bearing skill. The decoding process serves as a tool for the mental process when the reader tries to get meaning out of the printed material. Reading involves comprehension beyond decoding and literal level interpretations of the printed symbols. Reading is, in fact, a complex process and has so many facets that a simple definition cannot cover all of them. Effective reading includes experiencing, learning and thinking. The more complex the reader's task, the more he must give of his own experiences if he wants to derive satisfaction out of his reading activity.

REFERENCES

1. Waples, Douglas; Berelson, Bernard and Bradshaw, Franklin R. *What Reading Does to People,* University of Chicago Press, Chicago, III., 1940, pp. 144 and 30-31.
2. Ciardi, John. "The Well Read Man", in Albert J. Mazurkiewicz (ed) *New Perspectives in Reading Instruction,* Pitman Publishing Corp., New York, 1964, pp. 86-87.
3. Doren, Mark Van. "In Praise of Reading", *Explorations in Reading,* June, 1962.
4. Hafner, Lawrence E. *Improving Reading in Secondary Schools,* The Macmillan Company, New York, 1967, pp. 9-10.
5. Johns, J. L. "Reading: a View from the Child", *The Reading Teacher,* 28 (7), (1970), 647-48.
6. Ahuja, G. C. "Reading: As Viewed by Children", *Journal of Educational Research and Extension,* 11 (4), (April 1975), 225-27.
7. Ahuja, G. C. "Reading: As Viewed by the Teacher", *Educational India,* 41 (8), (February 1975), 184-85.
8. Ahuja, Pramila. "Reading: A Visual and Mental Phenomenon", *The Education Quarterly,* 27 (2), (July 1975), 23-25.
9. Betts, Emmett Albert. *Foundations of Reading Instruction,* American Book Company, New York, 1957, pp. 74-75, 75-76. and 79
10. Gray, William S and Others. *Reading in General Education,* American Council on Education, Washington, D. C., 1940, p. vii.
11. Artley, A. Sterl. *Your Child Learns to Read,* Scott, Foresman, Chicago: 1953, p. 7.

12. Russell, David H. "The Role in Pupil Development of a Sound Foundation in Reading", *Basic Instruction in Reading in Elementary and High Schools.* Supplementary Educational Monographs, No 65, University of Chicago Press, 1948, p. 8.

13. Gray, William S. "The Major Aspects of Reading", in Helen M. Robinson (ed.), *Sequential Development of Reading Abilities,* Supplementary Educational Monographs No. 90, University of Chicago Press, Chicago, 1960, pp. 13-19.

14. Robinson, Helen M. "The Major Aspects of Reading", in H. A. Robinson (ed.), *Reading Seventy-Five Years of Progress,* Supplementary Educational Monographs No. 96; University of Chicago Press, Chicago 1966, pp. 22-32.

15. Clymer, Theodore. "What is Reading? Some Current Concepts" in Helen M. Robinson (ed.), *Innovation and Change in Reading Instruction,* National Society for the Study of Education, Chicago, 1968, p. 29.

16. Reed, David W. "A Theory of Language, Speech, and Writing", *Elementary English,* 42 (1965), 845-51.

17. Soffietti, James P. "Why Children Fail to Read: A Linguistic Analysis," *Harvard Educational Review,* (Spring, 1955).

18. Goodman, Kenneth. "Reading: A Psycholinguistic Guessing Game", presented at the American Education Research Convention, New York City, February, 1967; mimeographed.

19. Wiener, Morton and Cromer, Ward. "Reading and Reading Difficulty: A Conceptual Analysis", *Harvard Educational Review,* 37, (1967), 620-43.

20. Harris, Albert J. *How to Increase Reading Ability,* David Mckay Company, Inc., New York, 1970, p. 7.

21. Russell, David H. *Children Learn to Read,* Ginn, Boston, 1949, p. 74.

22. Waples, Douglas. op, cit., 1940.

23. Horn, Ernest. *Methods of Instruction in the Social Studies,* Charles Scribner's Son, New York, 1937, p. 152.

24. Advisory Committee of Assistant Superintendents, Division of Elementary Schools, "Sequential Levels of Reading Growth in the Elementary School", New York City Schools, New York, Feb., 1963.

25. Betts, Emmett Albert. Foundations, op. cit.

26. Zahner, Louis C. "Approach to Reading Through Analysis of Meanings", *Reading and General Education,* American Council of Education, Washington, D. C., 1940, p. 77.

27. Anderson, Verna Dieckman. *Reading and Young Children,* The Macmillan Company, London, 1968. pp. 19-20.

28. Starng, Ruth. *Helping Your Child Improve His Reading,* Dutton, New York, 1962, p. 76.

29. Smith, F. *Understanding Reading,* Holt, Rinehart and Winston, New York, 1971.

30. Merritt, J. "Teaching Reading in Junior and Secondary Schools", *Teaching Reading: Ace Forum* 4, Ginn, London, 1970.

31. Betts, Emmett Albert. Foundations, op. cit.

2

SCIENCE OF READING

Is there such a thing like 'science of reading?' What is it? How does it work? What are its uses? How do we go in for studying the reading behaviour of an individual? Is there any difference in the way in which an adult performs the reading act and a child pursues the printed materials? Why do we consider reading a complex process? Is it altogether a covert behaviour? Is it an activity only meant for children or should adults also know about the reading process? Is there any difference in the way in which a fast reader and the way in which a slow reader pursues the line of print? Have we ever tried to think that without 'reading' we would not have been placed in the category of educated creatures?

Reading is man's most cogent skill. If we happen to place the mastery of reading on one pan of the balance, and all the other subjects on the other, the other will hit the beam. This very clearly shows the supremacy of 'reading' over all other subject areas of the curriculum. The statement 'he is a well read man' very well reflects the worth of reading.

Facets of reading are many. Reading is a physiological process, a psychological process, a social process, a cultural process and above all a linguistic process. It is an educational phenomenon. It has got its unique pedagogy.

To the perception psychologist,[1] reading is not an isolated behaviour that can be understood adequately by itself. Depending as heavily as it does on the language skills and on directed visual search, reading text, as a perceptuomotor activity, has certain characteristics in common with listening to speech and with viewing scenes. The first characteristic shared by these three activities, which is more obvious in the case of reading than in the other two, is that these behaviours do not consist of automatic responses to the array or sequence of patterned stimulation that confronts the subject. The reader does not merely regard a block of the text and immediately realise its message. He must intend to read the display, must "pay attention" to its meaning, if he is to be able to respond to its contents. What a phrase like "pay attention to" might mean in this context has not received much thought or experimental research, but it would seem to be of fundamental importance to any understanding of what the reading process is all about.

The act of reading can be both skilful and rewarding provided the reader sets out to read with a receptive mind. Reading ability and good reading habits have social significance as well as individual value. It is a personal affair which every person likes to perform in his own way. Many of us may not recall how or when we started to read. It may have been so much a part of our normal activities that there was no crucial moment when it began. Some of us may have a vivid memory of a certain teacher who taught us the beginnings of reading. Many of us may recall our experiences of sitting on our mother's or father's knee and being helped to read. Nevertheless, each of us learned to read. It was such an automatic activity for us that we never bothered about its mechanism. Now the times have changed and we have to change ourselves if we want to keep pace with the speed of change. Our society makes such heavy demands on the ability to read that each individual must learn to read efficiently. Even an interested reader cannot get any enlightenment from his reading unless he has full command over the mechanics of reading. It becomes very much necessary for a reader to know what the complex process of reading involves and how the eye works in reading.

Work of the Eye in Reading

The eye movement habits rather than mere visual efficiency determine the degree of reading efficiency.[2] It was Professor Javal of University of Paris who in 1879 gave us the idea that there are decided differences between the way poor readers read and the way an excellent reader pursues the printed page. Photographic studies of the eye movement in reading originated with the psychologists B. Erdman and Raymond Dodge at the University of Halle in Germany in 1898. Dr Guy T. Buswell of the University of Chicago was among the first to demonstrate the improvement as they matured in reading habits and to chart the direction of greater speed regularity and reduction in the number of fixations with improved comprehension.

The eyes move in a series of jerks and stops while the person is reading. Eyes jerk, they stop, they jump ahead in a speedy manner and stop. This process of 'move-stop', 'move-stop' makes the reading act possible. When a person reads, his eyes have to be fixated on some point because when they are moving a person cannot see. In order to see, the pauses which the eyes make are called 'fixations'. The amount of reading which a person does during one fixation is known as his 'span of recognition'. When the eye jumps from one fixation to another, it has to make a movement. This movement which the eye makes for going from one fixation to another is known as 'saccadic movement' or 'interfixation movement'. Sometimes it happens that when the person is not able to get the message out of his already made fixation or fixations, then a refixation is required. This refixation movement is called a 'regression'. Regressions are good if these are done to confirm certain details but if these are unduly large in number, they hinder the reading speed of a person. Habitual regressions are always bad. When a reader completes a line, his eye makes a movement at the end of the line, to go to the beginning of the next line, this movement is called a 'return sweep'. The eye nomenclatures have been elaborated below since these have got direct bearing on the reading process.

Fixation: At each fixation, the eye sees some letters according to the span of recognition of the reader. The duration of a fixation represents the time that the reader requires to perceive the printed symbols, to comprehend the meaning of the symbols, and to make certain associations before he proceeds to the next fixation.

Buswell[3] found that the average child in grade one made between 15.5 and 18.6 fixations per 3½ inch line. The average college student made only 5.9 fixations on a line of similar length.

Walker[4] studying the eye movements of 50 superior readers among freshmen at the University of Iowa, obtained an average of slightly more than eight fixations per four-inch line on material of moderate difficulty.

The duration and frequency of fixations vary with the difficulty level of the reading material and the reader's facility in word recognition, with his vocabulary level, with his familiarity with the content, with his purpose, with his ability to assimilate ideas, and with the format of the printed or the written page which also includes legible handwriting. But in general for an efficient reader, these fixations have a duration of 250 milliseconds (one-fourth of a second) or even 200 milliseconds (one-fifth of a second). An inefficient reader requires twice or even thrice as much of fixation time.

Tinker[5] suggests that the fixation varies from about 290 milliseconds (.22 seconds) for easy reading material, 236 milliseconds for scientific prose, and from 270 to 324 milliseconds for reading objective test items. Fixations account for approximately 92 to 94 per cent of the reading time, whereas eye-movement time accounts for about six to eight per cent of the reading time. The eyes tend to converge during the return sweeps and the interfixation movements, and to diverge during the fixation that follows.

Ledbetter,[6] studying the eye-movement records of 60 eleventh graders tested with 300-word selections from various fields, found that eye movements varied with the nature of the material. He found that comprehension also varied, and concluded that for the average student meanings are more crucial than vocabulary, sentence length, or sentence structure.

Tinker[7] summarises the past research on this point and concludes that as the difficulty of the material increases and as the individual takes greater pains to read well, the fixation pauses become more frequent and grow longer. In a later analysis[8] he points out that eye-movement patterns reflect the efficiency of the central processes of comprehension. He suggests that when eye movements do not vary with the difficulty of the reading matter, the readers are immature. Oculo-motor behaviour is a symptom of the underlying perceptual and assimilative processes. Efficient reading results in efficient eye movements rather than vice-versa.

Span of Recognition: The span of recognition is the amount of print seen during a single fixation. This extends equidistance on either side of the point of fixation. In the human eye, the field of vision is the area the eyes can see distinctly while they are fixed upon some given point. The field of clearest vision is the fovea in the centre of the eye. Macula is the area of the less distinct vision which surrounds the fovea. As the reader looks at the print, he sees some portions clearly and others vaguely in the marginal vision. Each fixation in succession brings new material into clear vision which was seen by the reader only vaguely.

The span of recognition averages 13 to 14 letter spaces (say about 3 words for good readers) and 6 spaces (say about 1 word) for poor readers. The size of the span of recognition can be obtained by dividing the length of the average line in the text read by the average number of fixations in a line. Span of recognition is also known as fixation span or eye span.

The wider the span of recognition, the better it is for faster reading but there is a physiological perceptual limit beyond which the eye cannot go. This is because of the way the eyes are set in the head.

Laycock[9] reports that the more flexible reader is distinguished from the less flexible reader both by his rate of eye movement and by the width of his fixation span. He used an experimental group of 37 college students who could shift their rate easily and a control group of 35 who had more difficulty in doing so. He felt that his evidence suggested that the rate of progression and width of the fixation span are the eye-movement characteristics that training programmes might best emphasise.

Interfixation Movement: This is the movement of the eye from one fixation to another. When the eyes move from one fixation to the other, clear vision of the print is not possible. This interfixation movement (or saccadic movement as it is sometimes called) is of very short duration lasting little over 1/100th of a second in the case of a mature reader (10 to 23 milliseconds each on an average). This very movement becomes comparatively larger in case of an immature reader. This activity of the eye when it goes from one fixation to another in quick succession can be compared with 'rope skipping' as is done by children while they are at play.

Regressions: Sometimes, the eyes move backwards to get a second look at some words which were not clearly seen. Such a backward movement is called a regression.

Regressive movements may be the result of many different causes. Among very poor readers, the most common cause of regression is failure to recognise a word, necessitating additional inspection of the word. Some other causes of regressions are failure to recognise the basic meaning of a word: failure to select the correct meaning of a word in the given context; inappropriate phrasing, spoiling the meaning and making rereading necessary; overlooking punctuation marks, confusing the meaning; inadequate perception resulting from an eye movement which overreaches the reader's span of perception; and external distraction which interrupts the reader's train of thought.[10]

Bayle[11] reports that regressions are likely to occur when the flow of thought is interrupted or when perceptions are recognised as inaccurate. The flow of thought may be broken in a number of ways; failure to recognise the basic meaning of a word; failure to recognise the meaning suggested by the context; failure to relate the meaning of one word to that of other words; or failure to relate the meaning of a word to the conditions under which it is used. Buswell reported that regressions result in immature reading but Bayle has suggested that a certain amount of regression is desirable. Regressions for verification, for phrase analysis, and for re-examination of a previous sentence seem especially useful. Taylor[12] found that senior high school students made on an average 15 regressions per 100 words and college students made 11. Gilbert[13] found that ninth-graders averaged 18.5 regressions per 100 words and college students made 13.6.

When researchers in reading first succeeded in recording eye movements, many concluded that to improve reading it was necessary to improve eye movements. The reasoning was that, generally, poor readers had many more regressions and required more fixations per line than did good readers. It seemed logical that if the number of regressions and fixations could be reduced, reading would be improved.[14]

Tinker[15] earlier questioned the desirability of attempting to improve reading through exercises designed to correct faulty eye movements. He believed that eye movements do not cause, but merely reflect efficient or poor reading performance. Hildreth[16] opines: there is nothing standardised about the regressive movements because these movements are governed by the difficulties, such as lack of word recognition and a shortage of vocabulary, encountered in reading. The number of the fixations and regressive movements appear to be little affected by fatigue except after reading of several hours' duration.

Return Sweep: As the term implies, this is a return movement of the eyes from the end of a line to the beginning of the next line. Tinker[17] says that the return sweep takes from 40 to 54 milliseconds. Inaccuracies here may require refixations. For example, the proper line may be missed entirely or the eye may fix on a point before or after the first word of the new line. Eye-movements during the reading of a line have been shown on Chart I, page 25.

Return sweep movement becomes part of the total reflex eye-movement pattern—brief, automatic and rhythmical through more and more reading practice. A fast reader takes very fast return sweeps involving even less than 40 milliseconds whereas a slow reader takes much more time ranging from 90 to 300 milliseconds.

The Anticipation Span/Eye-Voice Span

The classical term for the forward sweep of the eyes ahead of the point of interpretation is eye-voice span. This phenomenon was first described by J. O. Quantz in a study published by Princeton University late in 1897.[18] Quantz noted that in oral reading, interpretation of print lagged behind the forward sweep of the eyes. The length of this span was not difficult to detect in oral reading because the distance could be measured between the point reached by the eyes in a line and the point in the line at which the voice was enunciating the words. Quantz found a high correlation between reading rate and width of eye-voice span. In 1908, Dr E. B. Huey described 'forward push' of association expectancy, in which the eyes pick up words ahead of their interpretation. He noted that the great advantage in this characteristic was that it permitted an uninterrupted stream of interpretation at a rapid rate with minimum error.[19]

The eye-voice span or anticipation span as it is called ensures maximum speed and accuracy in interpretation whether it is oral reading task or silent reading task.

Buswell[20] points out an eye-voice span of considerable width necessary for intelligent grasp of the material read, and for reading orally with good expression.

Dr Buswell observed that when children failed to anticipate punctuation marks in oral reading they were totally unprepared for the voice expression required e.g., a rising inflection in the case of a question mark. A good oral reader with a wide A-span grasps meaning in terms of thought units, hence he reads expressively to his audience much as though he were speaking.

Hildreth[21] is of the opinion that the term eye-voice span is a misnomer for silent reading. In oral reading the A-span (anticipation span) is the distance between the point to which the eyes have moved ahead in the line and the point which the voice has reached in pronouncing; in silent reading, the distance between the point to which the eyes have moved ahead and the point at which interpretation is taking place ... During rapid silent reading the mind does not stop and wait as the eyes run on ahead; nor do the eyes suddenly stop at the end of a thought unit and wait for the mind to catch up. The whole process is so swift and fluent that a steam of thought moves steadily along, but it lags behind the progress of the eyes along the lines.

In general a mature reader's A-span in silent reading ranges between 15 to 20 letter spaces. Quantz called attention to the varying length of the eye-voice span depending on the part of the sentence being read—fore, middle, or end part. The eye-voice span is longest at the beginning and shortest at the ends of the lines.

For 54 subjects Buswell[22] reported the eye-voice span of 15.9 letter spaces at the beginning of the sentences, 13.4 in the middle, and 10.9 letter spaces at the end of sentences. This difference was more marked in the case of good readers.

Fairbanks[23] also found that the eye-voice span was shortest at the end of sentences, but he found no difference in spans in the beginning and middle of the sentences.

Why is this span shorter towards the end of the line? Hildreth[24] answers this question in this way: 'the span is shorter towards the end of the lines because the train of thought is momentarily disrupted. Fortunately, the breaks at the end of the lines do not constitute any marked disruption in the thought process because of the rapidity of the return sweep. The size of the span is also controlled by line length. There is a human limit to the size of the A-span just as there is to the size of the perception span, but in the case of the first the limitation is mental, a matter of attention, experience, familiarity, and memory; in the latter case, the limit is physiological.'

The significance of Eye Movements

Reading is a complex process which involves close interaction between the eye and the mind. The sequence of fixations across a line of print connotes the directional attack which a person uses while reading.

The quality of a person's directional attack is measured by dividing the number of regressions by the number of total fixations. The lower the percentage of regressions, the better the directional attack. The efficient reader spends less than 10 per cent of his time regressing, and the inefficient reader might spend as much as a third or more of his time regressing, 15 to 25 per cent being the average.[25]

The eye-movement study conducted to establish grade level norms for reading performance shows that the average college student, reading 280 words per minute, sees 1.1 words per eye stop. Eye-movement norms have been reported in Chart 2, page 27. Eye-movement studies of exceptional readers shows that they rarely see more than 2.5 to 3 words per eye stop.[26] One of the more significant differences between good and poor readers lies in the fact that good readers have developed an adequate span to recognition, as well as a systematic way of attacking each line of print. Poor readers have a narrower span of recognition and they are not aware of their directional attack. Poor readers also require more fixation time to see and react than do good readers.

Eye-movement recording, then, provides direct information about the reader's efficiency (the time and energy expended and the visual approach employed). It also provides indirect information about his effectiveness (his ability to accomplish expected comprehension goals).[27]

A study by Taylor and Robinson[28] suggests that a child enters kindergarten with certain existing oculo-motor habits born out of his accumulated "looking" experiences. These are modified or built upon as he learns to read.

Chart 1

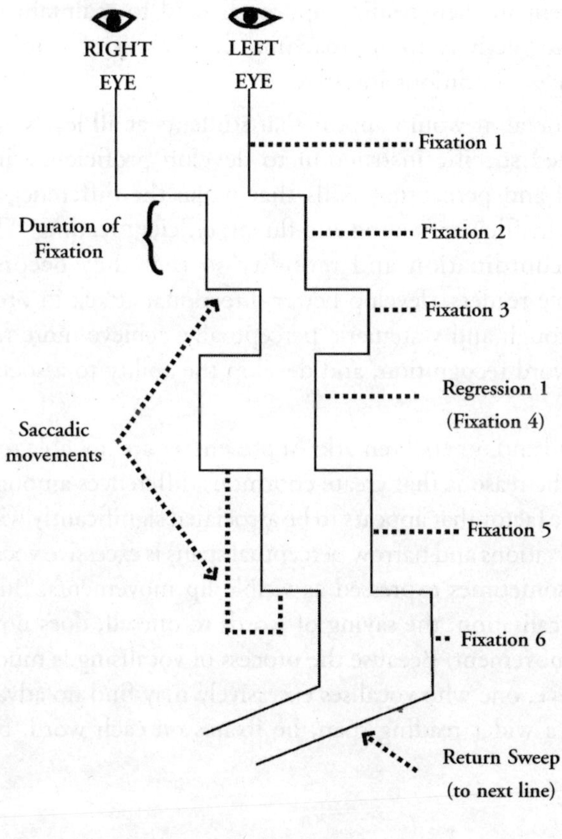

An inefficient reader habitually makes an excessive number of eye pauses per line, regresses very freely and tends to regard reading as a chore—a routine, slow and totally mechanical activity.

A very important question yet very much neglected in our day-to-day reading activity is—does an average individual alter his oculo-motor activity to suit the reading task? The probable answer can be 'Yes' and 'No'. While nobody denies that flexibility in reading is a desirable goal for each and every reader, the fact remains that the average reader is quite inflexible in the ways he manages with varied reading situations.

In a number of studies cited by Taylor,[29] it was found that only the better or more mature readers were able to alter their performance significantly when approaching different types of content with different purposes in mind. Average and below-average readers, who are not very efficient in their reading approach tend to maintain the same oculo-motor activity in approaching most types of reading unless extraordinary conditions interfere.

In general, it would appear that students at all levels, as well as adults, need specific instruction to develop proficiency in visual-functional and perceptual skills that make the difference between laborious, inefficient reading and fluent, efficient reading. They need to build coordination and mobility so that they become more comfortable readers, develop better directional attack in order to be more thorough and systematic perceptually, achieve more rapid and accurate word recognition, and develop the ability to associate more rapidly.[30]

Stroud and others[31] remark: At present we are not able to account for all of the reasons that create enormous differences among reading spans. One factor that appears to be associated significantly with word-by-word fixations and narrow perceptual spans is excessive vocalisation, which is sometimes expressed as visible lip movements. But a great deal of vocalisation, the saying of words to oneself, does not involve overt lip movement. Because the process of vocalising is much slower than the eye, one who vocalises excessively may find no advantage in achieving a wider reading span; he fixates on each word, or one or

Chart 2

Eye-Movement Norms*

Grade	1	2	3	4	5	6	7	8	9	10	11	12	College
Fixations per 100 words (including regressions)	224	174	155	139	129	120	114	109	105	101	96	94	90
Regressions per 100 words	52	40	35	31	28	25	23	21	20	19	18	17	15
Average Span of Recognition (in words)	.45	.57	.65	.72	.78	.83	.88	.92	.95	.99	1.04	1.06	1.11
Average Duration of fixations (in seconds)	.33	.30	.28	.27	.27	.27	.27	.27	.27	.26	.26	.25.	.24
Rate with Comprehension (words per minute)	80	115	138	158	173	185	195	204	214	224	237	250	280

* Taylor, Stanford E. Frackenpohl, Helen., and Pette James L., *Grade Level Norms for the Components of the Fundamental Reading Skill,* Research Information Bulletin, No. 3, Educational Developmental Laboratories, Huntington, New York, 1960, p. 12.

two words at a time, as though he were saying the words sub-vocally to himself. If you sub-vocalise in reading—entirely probable if you're a slow reader—try to compare introspectively your behaviour in reading and in listening. Except possibly in rare situations in which the exact words of a speaker are exceedingly important, do you feel a compulsion to repeat to yourself a speaker's words in order to understand them? Presumably some kind of neuromuscular reaction is necessary in all perception, thought, recall, or in the whole of mental life. But do we have to name an animal to know that it is a horse or a sheep, or an object of furniture to know that it is a chair? As just intimated, we do not have to repeat the words of a speaker in order to understand them. How necessary, therefore, is it to repeat the words of a writer in order to understand them?

One may say and rightly so—reading and listening are two different functions and for different functions we need not necessarily follow the same steps. Our own reaction to this may be that in spite of the fact that reading and listening are two different skills—they are here to lead us towards the same goal—understanding, *i.e.*, comprehension. The only difference is between the agents of different categories who send the message to the brain. In the case of reading, these are the visual symbols which serve as the message sent through the medium of eye as the messenger to the brain. In the case of listening, the message in the form of the spoken words is sent through the medium of the ear as the messenger to the brain. Since reading is an individual affair, the speed at which the message is sent to the brain depends on the individual whereas in listening the person has to depend on the speaker's speed over which the listener does not have any control. Whatever the case may be, the ultimate aim is comprehension.

While Kainz[32] believes that the highly skilled reader proceeds directly from the printed symbol on the page to the underlying concept, that the printed word itself is a carrier of meaning, many studies show that even the fluent reader evokes the auditory and motor images symbolised by letters, but that these images are so fleeting and of so short a duration that the individual is not necessarily aware of them. Even the practised reader will resort to vocalisation when he meets an unknown word or tries to understand a difficult passage.

Inner speech phenomena are probably never entirely eliminated. How many vocal clues are needed may be a matter of reading proficiency.

Reading Ability Is Transferred from One Language to Another

Reading ability is a general power. It is not confined to one language: for improvement in the ability to read one language is "transferred", and shows itself in improvement of the reading of another language. Thus a class of seventeen-year-old Bengali students were given twenty periods of practice aiming at increased speed and efficiency in the reading of English; the practice was given entirely in English. The resulting improvement in the rate of English reading was 232 per cent, while the improvement in the rate of Bengali reading (in which no practice had been given) was 266 per cent.[33]

What about the eye movements in the conventional printed page of other languages, *e.g.*, Hebrew and Urdu in which the print goes from right to left, and in Chinese which goes up the columns vertically?

Gray[34] made a survey of eye movements in reading foreign languages. Seventy-eight mature subjects read material in their mother-tongue in 14 different languages. The material used was an old fable common to all of these languages except the Navaho (native American Indian) and a simple discussion of reasons why children and adults should learn to read and write. The results of two tests in both silent and oral reading showed striking similarity in the character of the eye movements in all languages. Gray concluded that reading patterns around the world were essentially the same regardless of the form and structure of a particular language or orientation of the lines of print.

A person who reads English fluently can read Urdu also fluently provided his background in the two languages is the same.

SUMMARY

Studies in the area of reading behaviour have shown that the human eye traverses the print in the lines by a series of movements and pauses. There is a movement, then a pause, again a movement, then a pause;

and so on until the line is completed. Eye movements are characterised by fixations, interfixations, regressions and return sweeps. The amount of printed material or the number of words which a person perceives during each fixation is called his span of recognition. The wider the span of recognition, the lesser the number of fixations tend to be.

The sequence of fixation across a line of print connotes the directional attack which a person uses while reading. The quality of a person's directional attack is measured by dividing the number of regressions by the number of total fixations. The lower the percentage of regressions, the better the directional attack. The efficient reader possesses a better directional attack. He spends less than 10 per cent of his reading time regressing, and the inefficient reader might spend as much as a third or more of this time regressing. Reading skills can be improved by training. Being a general skill, it can be improved with systematic training and it has got transfer value. Reading patterns around the world are essentially the same regardless of the form and structure of a particular language or orientation of the lines of print.

REFERENCES

1. Hochberg, Julian and Brooks, Virginia. "Reading as an Intentional Behaviour", in Larry A. Harris and Carl B. Smith., *Individualizing Reading Instruction: A Reader,* Holt, Rinehart and Winston, Inc., New York, 1972, p. 50.
2. Hildreth, Gertrude. *Teaching Reading,* Holt, Rinehart and Winston, New York, 1958 (reprinted May 1965), pp. 65, 70, 76-77, 80.
3. Buswell, G. T. *Fundamental Reading Habits: A Study of their Development,* Supplementary Educational Monographs, No. 21, University of Chicago Press, Chicago, 1922, p. 26.
4. Walker, Robert Y. "The Eye-Movement of Good Readers", *Studies in Experimental and Theoretical Psychology,* Psychological Monograph, No. 3, 44 (1933), 95-117.
5. Tinker, Miles A., in Leonard, Carmichael., and Water, F. Dearborn., *Reading and Visual Fatigue,* Houghton-Mifflin Company, Boston, 1947.
6. Ledbetter, Frances Gresham. "Reading Reactions for Varied Types of Subject Matter; An Analytical Study of the Eye Movements of Eleventh Grade Pupils", *Journal Educational Research,* 41 (October 1947), 102-115.
7. Tinker, Miles A. "Time Relations for Eye-Movement Measures in Reading", *Journal of Educational Psychology,* 38, (January 1947), 1-10.
8. Tinker, Miles A. "Recent Studies of Eye Movements in Reading", *Psychological Bulletin,* 55 (July 1958), 215-231.
9. Laycock, Frank. "Significant Characteristics of College Students with Varying Flexibility in Reading Rate: 1. Eye-Movements in Reading prose", *Journal of Experimental Education,* 23 (June 1955), 311-19.

10. Harris, Albert J. *How to Increase Reading Ability,* David Mckay Company, Inc., New York, 1970, p. 492.

11. Bayle, Evalyn. "The Nature and Causes of Regressive Movements in Reading", *Journal of Experimental Education,* 11 (September 1942), 16-36.

12. Taylor, Earl A. *Bulletin of the Washington Square Reading Centre,* New York, 1954.

13. Gilbert, Luther C. *Functional Motor Efficiency of the Eyes and Its Relations to Reading,* Publications in Education, No. 3, University of California Press, 1953, 159-232.

14. Smith, Henry P and Dechant, Emerald V. *Psychology in Teaching Reading,* Prentice-Hall International, Inc., London, 1961, p. 126.

15. Tinker, Miles A. "The Use and Limitations of Eye-Movement Measures in Reading", *School and Society,* 39 (February 1934), 147-148.

16. Hildreth, Gertrude. *Teaching Reading ...* op. cit.

17. Tinker, Miles A. "Recent Studies ... op. cit.

18. Quantz, J. O. *Problems in the Psychology of Reading,* Psychological Review Monograph Supplement, Psychological Review Co. Princeton, N.J., 2 (1), (1897).

19. Huey, E. B. *The Psychology and Pedagogy of Reading,* Macmillan, New York, 1908.

20. Buswell, Guy T. *An Experimental Study of the Eye-Voice Span in Reading,* Supplementary Educational Monographs, No. 17, University of Chicago Press, Chicago, 1920.

21. Hildreth, Gertrude. *Teaching Reading ...* op. cit.

22. Buswell, Guy T. *An Experimental Study ...* op. cit.

23. Fairbanks, Grant. "The Relation Between Eye-Movements and Voice in the Oral Reading of Good and Poor Silent Readers", *Psychological Monographs,* 48 (3), (1937), Studies in the Psychology of Reading 1, University of lowa Studies in Psychology, No. 21.

24. Hildreth, Gertrude. *Teaching Reading ...* op. cit.

25. Taylor, Stanford E and Frackenpohl, Helen. *Teacher's Guide: Controlled Reading,* EDL., McGraw-Hill, Inc., New York, 1970, pp. 6, 7, 10.

26. Spache, George D. *Is this a Breakthrough in Reading?* EDL Research and information Reprint No. 4 EDL, Inc., Huntington, New York, 1962.

27. Taylor, Stanford E and Robinson, Alan H. "The Relationship of the Oculo-Motor Efficiency of the Beginning Reader to His Success in Learning to Read", A paper presented at the American Educational Research Association Conference, February 13-16, 1963.

28. Taylor, Stanford E and Robinson, Alan H. "The Relationship of ... op. cit.

29. Taylor, Stanford E. "Eye-Movements and Reading: Facts and Fallacies", *American Educational Research Journal,* 2 (November 1965), 187-202.

30. Taylor, Stanford E and Frackenpohl, Helen. *Teacher Guide ...* op. cit.

31. Stroud, James Robert B; Ammons, B and Bamman, Henry A. *Improving Reading Ability,* Appleton-Century-Crofts, Educational Division, Meredith Corporation, New York, 1970, pp. 6-7.

32. Kainz in Lawrence E. Hafner, *Improving Reading in Secondary Schools: Selected Readings,* The Macmillan Company, New York, 1967, p. 461.

33. West, Michael. *Learning to Read a Foreign Language,* Longmans, London, 1960, p. 7.

34. Gray, W. S. "Reading Problems that Merit International Study", *UNESCO Educational Studies and Documents,* No. 20, UNESCO, Paris, 1956, 41-47.

3

DEVELOPING GREATER SPEED IN READING

"Reading", in the words of Francis Bacon, "maketh the full man"—and this neatly epitomises the goal of reading instruction. The ability to read is a foundation for success and growth. We want to learn to read so that we may be in a position to enrich our lives with a vast amount of knowledge. We want to read rapidly because in no other manner can we so readily share the experiences of the rest of mankind. The more one reads, the better informed is one regarded.

Reading is the torch that lights the mind. It can generate both heat and light. It may produce searing heat which fuses ideas, or light that almost blinds through illumination of thought and feeling. Yet a flaming torch may also produce destruction and, by analogy, reading may have abuses and uses.[1]

David Russell once said that a writer only begins a book. It is the reader who completes it. The reader takes what he can from the printed pages, but it is the thoughts and feelings that are stirred up within the reader that carry him beyond the mere print. A book, whether it be written for children or adults, is only as good as the effect it has on the reader.[2]

We react to reading intellectually, emotionally, aesthetically, and with value judgements, with varying degrees of feeling in each case.[3]

You can well recall many incidents in the books which made you almost shed tears.

What a person reads is as important as how well he reads it.

There is a story of a centipede who had no problem travelling about until he thought about which leg he would move next while engaged in walking. The centipede's experience might lead us to guess that by continually thinking about eye movements while actually reading will not lead to more effective reading. However, understanding how the eyes function in the process of reading could lead to an insight as to what can be done to achieve more effective reading habits.[4]

If as an adult, you are using inefficient reading habits, it is obvious that more and more reading will not automatically result in improved reading skills. The more you read the more you reinforce whatever habits you now have. This will be true unless you make some systematic effort to eliminate the existing habits which stand between you and efficient reading. You cannot rid yourself of habits which you have practised thousands of times simply by resolving to do so. This is true regardless of the sincerity of your resolution.[5]

Barriers to Speed-reading

Inefficient reading habits come in the way of rapid reading and act as barriers to one's reading speed. The most common barriers are:

1. Faulty visual perception
2. Word by word reading
3. Regressions
4. Finger pointing and head swinging
5. Vocalisation
6. Sub-vocalisation
7. Lack of stamina
8. Lack of motivation and reading interests
9. Other miscellaneous barriers

These have been discussed in detail in the following pages.

Faulty Visual Perception: Some readers, even though their vision may be perfect, have a visual perception problem which causes faulty recognition of words. They may mistake such words as pilot for plot, residence for resistance, stalk for stick, ladder for latter, or in some extreme cases, was for saw. Because many words have the same basic configuration, they tend to cause problems for some readers.[6] It is not uncommon to find people making mistakes between similar words such as shore for sure, convenience for conveyance, etc. These habits create problems not only in reading but also affect one's writing. Drills in rapid word recognition skills may help a lot in this type of speed barrier. There are some readers who have difficulty with the return sweep. When they go from one line to another, they look back along the line and then drop vertically to the beginning of the next line. This habit is faulty and takes double the time which results in slow speed.

When difficulty in making the return sweep is discovered, one should look for evidence of eye-muscle difficulty or slow fusion, which at reading distance sometimes is a result of uncorrected farsightedness. To develop greater skill in making the return sweep, which should be a single quick diagonal movement, one can use widely spaced lines, with diagonal lines connecting the end of each line with the beginning of the next line.[7] A few days of practice will be sufficient to get rid of this barrier.

Word by Word Reading: One who reads word by word is positively a slow reader. Neither is he able to show reading speed nor comprehension of the read matter. He just becomes a word caller. Since he is not used to grasping the print in longer meaningful units, he cannot dare go faster. In fact, he is such a reader who is unable to see the forest because of the trees. He cannot anticipate meanings and, therefore, fails to make use of context clues. As a result he even makes unnecessary errors in word recognition which means still slowing down. These readers may be helped to get rid of this barrier by giving them practice on rapid phrase recognition exercises. They should be advised, therefore, to take more words in one fixation for widening their span of recognition. Taking material in larger, meaningful and thoughtful units will go a long way in getting rid of this barrier.

Try to read the following sentence aloud, a word at a time, pronouncing each word with the same tone:

If/a/person/reads/very/slowly,/word/by/word,/he/will/be/classified/as/an/inefficient/reader/even/though/he/may/do/well/on/comprehension.

Now read it with the following breaks:

If a person/reads very slowly/word by word/he will be/classified as/an inefficient reader/even though/he may/do well/on comprehension.

When one is reading word by word, it becomes necessary to keep in mind a large number of word symbols along with their relationships to each other. With this practice even if one knows the meanings of each and every word, he cannot get the meaning of the sentence. It means the eyes and mind must select the most logical phrasing possible, otherwise the meaning may become obscured.

Reading groups of words that fall together in speech as units help develop speed. If a reader stops worrying about the mechanics of reading and attends more carefully to meaning which is the ultimate goal in reading, he can go faster. The development of efficient reading speed (as opposed to word by word) is not at all difficult but requires practice.

Think of how you listen to someone who is talking to you. Somehow, all at the same time, you take in the tone of the voice, the speed with which he or she is talking, the rhythm of his or her language, the gesture he or she is making, the words themselves, and the meaning of what is being said. The entire process happens too quickly and immediately for you to hear words or even phrases separately. The whole of the act of speech is understood at one time. To prove this to yourself try to concentrate on each individual word in a conversation. Then try to concentrate on groups of words. Then on rhythm, etc. As you pay attention to one component you will most likely lose sight of the meaning of the whole.[8]

Regressions: A regression denotes backward movement along a line of print. This is a reverse movement from right to left. While regressing, the reader re-reads certain words or phrases in the line second time while following reverse eye movements. It is the same as return sweep which a reader makes after he has finished reading one line. Regressions or regressive movements as these are called sometimes, are the eye-movements equivalent of repetitions in oral reading. If one regresses very freely, it is a sign of poor reading. Sometimes when the reader is faced with a new or difficult word and wants to confirm its meaning with the help of context by a second review, a regressive movement is justifiable, but habitual use of regressions is bad.

When regressions are due to deficiencies or inaccuracies in word recognition or word meaning, attempting to train the eye movements will obviously be of little or no value. Any reader, no matter how skilful, will make a large number of regressions when reading material which is heavily loaded with unfamiliar words, peculiar or highly involved sentence structure, or very difficult ideas. However, if a tendency to excessive regressions persists as a lingering bad habit in a reader whose word recognition and comprehension are at a high level, specific exercises to overcome the regressions may be advisable.[9] Reading practice on very easy material will help a lot thus reducing the effect of his barrier.

Finger pointing and Head Swinging: Finger pointing holds the reader down to reading one word at a time. As a result only a very slow speed of reading can be attained. Finger cannot move as fast as the eye can see. Finger pointing by itself does not interfere with speed of reading or comprehension for that matter, but it is often an accompaniment of excessive word analysis resulting in speed break. The important factor on which to concentrate while reading is the idea that the author is trying to stress, and not the location of the words on the page which are being finger pointed. A card or a thick slip of paper held under the line of print as a marker serves as a good step in doing away with finger pointing.

Head swinging for going from one fixation to another or from one line to another prevents fast reading. Many adults move their heads from left to right and again from right to left each time they read a line. This is no good. This activity is very much fatiguing and in no way helps fast moving of the eyes. Many readers believe that head movement aids swift reading. This is absolutely wrong because our eye muscles are quite capable of shifting the eyes from word to word or one fixation to another and they do not need any help from neck muscles. When we attempt to read material from a book which is being shaken due to the bus being in motion, in that situation how difficult it becomes for the eyes to make head movements. It is tiring for the individual and at the same time interfixation movements require comparatively more time. Getting conscious about this barrier and practising reading without making use of head movement will be of help to the reader.

Vocalisation: It is not very uncommon to see readers in the libraries or in trains or at bus stops who are moving their lips or even murmuring while reading silently. This is called vocalisation. Vocalisation reduces the speed of a reader to the extent of his speaking speed which is less than 150 or 200 words per minute. The persistence of the habit of forming each word with lips and tongue hinders the growth of adequate speed in reading. Silent reading must be something other than inaudible oral reading. Studies have shown that vocalisation is a handicap for speed-reading purposes. This not only hinders speed, but also affects comprehension.[10]

As the silent reading of most normal reader is approximately twice as fast as their speaking and when the reader vocalises while reading he does not go beyond half of his silent reading speed which wastes double of his time.

Vocalisation may take various forms. Sometimes a reader merely moves his lips without making any sound. At other times he makes tongue or throat movements without lip movement. At still other times he will have activity going on in his vocal cords, which can be detected by the reader himself if he places his fingers alongside his larynx (vocal cords in the throat) while he is reading. Vocal cord vibration can be felt with the fingers quite easily.

Sub-Vocalisation: Sub-vocalisation is a severe type of vocalisation. In this type, there is no body movement—lips, tongue or vocal cords do not move at all but some form of inner speech goes on. It appears as if the reader is saying each word to himself—as if he is pronouncing each word and listening to himself—say a type of inner speech and inner hearing too. Inner speech and inner hearing have been reported often by many readers and these greatly affect their reading speed.

There is considerable argument among reading specialists and psychologists whether or not thought is of a verbal nature. Many claim that in all thinking some type of verbalisation occurs in the mind. Some experimentations have even attempted to show tiny traces of physiological correlates, such as movement of the tongue while reading. No matter whether there are or are not slight physiological correlates or vocalisation in all reading, we do know that the greater the amount of sub-vocalisation (the closer it approaches actual vocalisation), the lower the speed of reading. Students should be enjoined to read faster and to concentrate on the author's ideas and not to go through the motions of having an "internal radio announcer reading each word."[11]

Your mind and eye can work several times as fast as your lips or throat muscles to your 'inner hearing'. That means as long as you move your lips or have any throat activity, you cannot become a fast reader. If your lips move, they slow you down to not more than 150 words a minute. You cannot move your lips faster than that and it is very tiring to try to read even this fast. The same can be said for the throat muscles. Some people move these while reading. They do not know it and usually refuse to believe that they do, but they do it all the same, and this makes it impossible for them to read as fast as the eye and mind are capable of reading. Almost equally as bad a habit is that of making yourself mentally hear what you read. This mental hearing also slows you down. You do not need to hear even mentally (inner hearing). Reading should be by seeing and thought-getting alone. If you have any one of these three habits (lip moving, inner speech or inner hearing), it is absolutely essential that you break yourself of them before you can make progress in faster reading. An ox-cart and a motor car cannot travel in company unless the motor car slows down to suit the ox-cart. Similarly, good eye-movements and the three habits just mentioned cannot travel together without the eye slowing itself down to one-fourth its capacity.[12]

A direct attack on sub-vocalisation is not always successful. Sometimes when students first become aware of the fact that they are sub-vocalising (and this is true in most cases of people reading at speeds of less than 250 words a minute), they try to stop sub-vocalising by sheer willpower. They simply say to themselves, 'I will not sub-vocalise'. Often when the student does this he tends to stop understanding, whereas before, when he was sub-vocalising and saying each word inwardly to himself, he was at least taking in the story. But when he tries by dint of willpower to shut off all sub-vocalisation he may not understand a thing. His eyes may go across the print while nothing happens. As one student expressed it to me, 'the silence was killing me'. If this happens the student should be told to concentrate on the other aspects of reading, namely speed and comprehension. If he must talk to himself while reading let him say, 'What does this mean?', 'I don't believe this', 'This "point" is not related to the paragraph', or 'I'll bet this will be a question on the comprehension test'. In short, he should talk "about" the material but not repeat the words. He should in fact get mentally engaged in a conversation with the author, instead of merely parroting what the author says. Efficient reading requires an active mind, not the mere passivity of saying the author's words ... The negative approach of 'I will not sub-vocalise' should be replaced by the more positive attitudes of 'I must understand what the author is saying' and 'I must go faster'.[13]

Moreover, in the initial stages when the reader is practising faster reading, he should take very easy and interesting material which permits him to go very fast thus not allowing time for sub-vocalisation and gradually eliminating the need for it. However, while reading when one comes across an unfamiliar or difficult word, there arises a need to utter the word by mouth and that is not a sign of bad reading.

Lack of Stamina : Some people do not like reading. They even avoid coming into contact with well read people. They do not like the very smell of books. If sometimes by chance they have to go to the library for some work, they feel a type of suffocation. Meet Mr X who is a voracious reader and who loves to consume book after book from the library racks. And here is Mr Y who will never be seen in the library, he will never think of going inside the library to see the books even for the sake of seeing. There are people who have no stamina to speak of reading. Reading is a tiring activity for them.

Most people get tired after reading for several hours. Their heads spin, concentration disappears, they feel tired and almost physically exhausted. It is amazing how much physical energy can be expended while sitting still, looking and thinking. This statement may seem absurd until you think that a chess champion like Bobby Fischer can lose between five and ten pounds in a two-hour chess game and has to train hard, physically, for a chess match as a boxer does for a prize fight.[14]

Those who don't read can never build up any stamina. One has to make a beginning at some stage. After a good beginning has been made, it is possible to suggest that people push themselves a bit further every day. It is a gradual and painstaking task. Slowly and steadily it will be possible to get used to reading.

Another way to build stamina is to have people re-read favourite books in larger and larger sections at one sitting.

After all reading is a skill which can be developed with continuous and systematic practice. Speed is only one aspect of physical conditioning for reading. One learns to read with reasonable speed by reading alone. Do you remember the days in summer, when due to intense heat, the hand-pump dries out. You have to first put water in the pump, and then by pumping again, water starts flowing. Similar is the case with reading. Stamina for reading is something which the reader has to develop for himself but it will not be a problem once he decides to vote in favour of it.

Rabindranath Tagore had very rightly pointed out: 'The worm thinks it foolish that man does not eat his books.'

Some people love books. They want to possess a good number of books, spend a lot of money on purchasing them, preserve them in beautiful cupboards and take great care of them. Books are their priced possession, but to our great surprise, many of them are not readers. They take great delight in just watching them, securely and beautifully kept aside.

Lack of Motivation and Reading Interests: An interested reader is a motivated reader and a motivated reader is a voracious reader for whom 'reading' forms a major part of his daily diet. For a motivated reader 'reading' is as natural as breathing. He wants that he should be served with books at his breakfast table, in the garden when he is relaxing and on the bed when he is about to sleep. Reading becomes so much a part of his personality that it is difficult to separate the two.

It is a well recognised fact of psychology that habits are formed through the repetition of some act that satisfies a motivating condition. However, once well formed, habits no longer need draw on other motives for energy. They acquire their own ability to energise themselves. A child learns to read because he is motivated by basic, personal needs. But gradually, as he becomes skilled in reading, reading acquires a motivating force of its own.[15]

Allport[16] points out that a skill learned for some extraneous reason can turn into an interest and become self-propelling, even though the original reason for acquiring it may have been lost.

Getzels[17] defines an interest as "... a characteristic disposition, organised through experience, which impels an individual to seek out particular objects, activities, understanding, skills, or goals for attention or acquisition."

Interest patterns represent learned tendencies to respond selectively, positively, and with attendant satisfactions to particular contents, or opportunities in one's environment. These tendencies, for example, may induce a person to participate eagerly in a certain form of sport or play, a hobby or in reading an unusual book. Interests ordinarily induce pleasant anticipation followed by the action itself, which in turn tends to bring more pleasure. One whose interest has been awakened plays basketball, another goes swimming frequently, a third views a favourite television programme, or the same may participate in all these activities at different times. Usually a child or adult will tire quickly of an interest in which his activity becomes restricted or in which he can do nothing at all, though unsatisfied longings may persist.[18]

Attitudes and interests are closely related. Attitudes represent general predispositions, and specific interests operate within this broader sphere. Sometimes interests are defined as positive attitudes towards objects or classes of objects to which we are attracted.[19]

An interest may be classified either as a trait or as an attitude, depending, largely, on whether it is broad or narrow in its reference. At any rate, interests are "learned" responses which predispose the organism to certain lines of activity and which definitely facilitate "attention". A trait or an attitude may favour activity of a given sort without involving the clear awareness and concentrated activity involved when we are paying attention to something.[20]

Interests are learned. They arise from the interaction of our basic needs and the means that we discover for satisfying them. Interest in reading parallels learning how to read.[21] As william James suggested, "Only what we partly know already inspires us with a desire to know more."[22]

Lack of interest in the reading activity itself makes one a slow reader and the person who is not motivated to do certain reading becomes responsible for hindering his own reading speed. The potential for reading is there and he can go fast but due to lack of interest he has become slow.

Witty[23] reports a study of 100 boys and girls at the North-western University Laboratory. All were poor readers. Eighty-two showed a lack of interest in reading, and of these, 43 actually disliked reading. Other than lack of interest, he found few reasons for the poor reading. Only 14 had defective vision, three had defective hearing, and four were left-handed.

Nemoitin[24] studied the performance of 150 high school seniors and found a "substantial and marked relationship" between ability and interest. High interest in a subject tended to be associated with high ability in that subject, and low interest with low ability. Bernstein[25] reports that high interest in a subject is often associated with superior reading comprehension in that subject. She concluded that higher interest results in more creative responses or responses that show that pupils are reading actively and thinking about the material.

As a person learns to read, reading enters his mental make up as a permanent mode of behaviour ... Henceforth he uses reading as a means of enjoyment and as a means of studying and thinking. To the extent that he can read with ease, reading is a major factor in the control of his behaviour. He will often arrange his daily schedule of work and play in order to provide time for reading. He will make sacrifices in order to provide himself with books to read. He will turn to reading as a means of discovering new interests and of losing himself for a time from the actualities of the external world. It is at this point that we see the employment of advanced spontaneous attention. No longer is reading an end on the outside that conflicts with other tendencies. It is now a dominating interest that is within.[26]

We now recognise that "... to increase reading skill, promote the reading habit, and produce a generation of booklovers, there is no other factor so powerful as interest."[27]

There is always a tendency for interesting materials to be understood better than uninteresting material. It is hard to keep one's mind on dull content. Schnayer[28] had sixth-grade pupils read a number of stories that were two grades above the pupil's reading level. The children rated the stories for the interest and answered questions about them. There were three main findings: (*a*) interest in a selection may allow students of average ability to read and comprehend material that is above their measured reading level; (*b*) low interest has a negative effect on comprehension; and (*c*) the comprehension of high ability students is less affected by interest than that of average or low ability students.

This should not lead to the conclusion that if a selection is sufficiently interesting for a particular reader, its difficulty automatically goes off. The point is that interest of the reader in the selection makes the difficulty aspect mild for him and he is able to speed up.

Other Miscellaneous Barriers: The other barriers are word blocking, word analysis, monotonous plodding, back-tracking, re-reading, readability, mode and purpose, and lack of concentration. These are enumerated below:

(a) Word Blocking: Stopping to worry about an unfamiliar word breaks the tone and rhythm of the reader. This may be due to poor vocabulary. Instead of stopping over an unfamiliar word, one should take help of the context clues while reading, and go ahead. Afterwards the exact meaning may be seen from the dictionary. When the reader keeps worrying over the unfamiliar word, his chain of thought is missed which again affects the reading speed.

(b) Word Analysis: Some people are in the habit of stopping over some words to analyse them of their origin, structure, prefixes and suffixes. No doubt, this serves as a sound vocabulary building exercise but it takes the reader away from the context in which they are used. As a result more time of the reader is wasted.

(c) Monotonous Plodding: One who always reads at the same speed with all kinds of reading materials, cannot be called an efficient reader. To show efficiency in reading, one needs a flexible speed. Good readers may read at a very slow rate if they want a detailed understanding, but read at a very fast speed while reading story books or other recreational materials. When the reader just keeps plodding, his speed is hindered and comprehension lowered.

(d) Back-tracking: Going back to read some words again is an indication that the reader is doubting his ability to pick out the important material. As a result, he keeps thinking over the back ideas instead of accelerating his reading speed further.

(e) Re-reading: Lack of self-confidence or interruption in the reading assignment compels the reader to re-read the whole matter. Studies have shown that re-reading is a fairly ineffective method of reviewing immediately after study.

(f) Readability: Readability is also important as a factor essential for reading speed. A page which is not readable can obscure and produce visual discomfort and fatigue. Many factors are involved in determining the legibility of a printed page. These factors include the size of the type, the typeface, the length of the printed line, the paper and the ink used in the printing of the page, the kind and size of the illustrations and the presence or absence of decorations on the page margins. These aspects cover the external readability.

Internal readability of the reading materials in the form of comprehension levels also affects the reading speed of an individual. The reader will only be able to understand the reading material if it is in conformity with his level of reading development. The reading materials may be of three levels—Independent, Instructional, and

Frustrating. Researches have shown that for the reading materials to be suitable for use in a supervised instruction (instructional level), the student should be able to answer at least 75 per cent of the questions asked about the materials and that the materials be suitable for use in the student's independent study (independent level), he should be able to answer 90 per cent of the questions. When the reader shows 50 per cent or less comprehension, the reading material is considered to be of frustration level. One can read faster only when the material is of independent level. Any attempt to read difficult materials with a faster rate will yield disastrous results.

(g) Mode and Purpose: The mode and purpose of reading also affect the proficiency of the person who is reading. If the reader needs to get only a general impression or a general idea or if he merely needs to look up a given item on a page, the speed needs to be relatively high. But if he needs to grasp the concepts in a given selection thoroughly, his pace needs to be comparatively slow. This emphasises the need for purposeful reading. Prior to reading any unit, the reader should be clear as to the purpose for which he is going to read. The most satisfactory purpose is one stated by the reader himself.

(h) Lack of Concentration: Inability to concentrate well is a real problem among slow readers and it needs to be tackled very carefully. Lack of concentration hinders reading speed and consequently reading comprehension is lowered. It is necessary to learn to pay attention to the reading material. One must develop a strong sense of personal involvement. Unless one really wants to read something, concentration is bound to wander.

Concentration problems are as varied as individuals. Inability to concentrate can be caused by lack of interest in the reading matter, by lack of motivation, by attempting to read difficult material, by not being prepared to read, by being too tired, by noises, by emotional problems, by financial problems—in short by anything which distracts you. Even though your mind drifts to something other than what you are reading, you are still concentrating on that something. What you need to learn is a way to maintain your attention on your reading material ... As long as you are reading something you really want to read, your attention generally will remain focused. But when you are reading an assignment that you consider dull, you actually welcome and look for distractions. If you are not interested in what you are reading at the moment, you are probably finding it difficult. This may be because you did not prepare yourself to read this chapter by focusing on it first. It may be that you are tired. If so, you should postpone reading this until later. It may be that you do not really want to read faster but you just think you do. In other words, if you aren't really interested or properly motivated or properly "focused", you must expect poor concentration.[29]

Practising Speed-reading

Speed-reading practice is suitable only for those individuals whose word recognition, vocabulary, and comprehension are already adequate. Deficiencies in any of these areas should be remedied before time pressures are imposed. Under pressure, many sluggish habits with use of speed barriers are automatically discarded. Rapid reading selections for practice should include few unfamiliar words.

If vocabulary is meagre, reading will be an obstacle. A student can hardly profit from covering a page rapidly if he does not know the meanings of the words on the page. Instruction in skills of comprehension may be necessary before speed can be increased. Until the student has the sub-structure or essential skills, pressurising him to build faster rates of reading may be futile and probably harmful.[30]

Regular and systematic practice with very easy, highly interesting material, read for less exacting purposes, is a natural, effective means of increasing rates. The reading material should be of independent level and in no case should present any vocabulary or comprehension problems. The reader should be forced to be pulled along by intense interest. Exciting, fast-moving stories and narrative style biographies, rather than books on educational and informative essays which are usually heavily loaded with words and thoughts, are quite appropriate to begin with for developing a taste for faster reading. Books matching individual interest will prove to be very much useful for increasing speed of reading.

It is very important to encourage the reader to do a large amount of reading on interesting and easy material. A story or a novel of a kind that the reader enjoys is most suitable for this purpose since the desire to find out what will happen next automatically provides motivation to read at a fairly fast rate. Some readers fail to develop the rapid reading habits because most of their reading practices have been on the material which was difficult for them. Nothing except dissatisfaction will be achieved if the reading material is loaded with new, bombastic words and unfamiliar concepts. Speed and fluency develop naturally as a result of much practice in reading fairly easy, interesting, exciting, narrative and new reading material over which one has not to be examined. Reading such materials merely for enjoyment and recreation helps in building confidence in one's abilities to read faster.

Adams[31] forwards the following suggestions for practising speed-reading:

(*a*) Decide if you "really" want to work at increasing your rate.

(*b*) Set aside "at least" thirty minutes or more each day for practice reading.

(*c*) Try to establish a particular time of day for practice so that it soon becomes a regular part of your normal schedule.

(*d*) Do not practise when you are tired. You need to be alert to read well.

(*e*) Select reading materials from a variety of sources: newspapers, magazines, novels. The reading material should not be something you will be tested on.

(*f*) Read the material as rapidly as you can. Do not get bogged down in unfamiliar vocabulary or writing styles at first.

(*g*) Expect some drop in your present level of comprehension. When you begin to read faster than normal you cannot maintain high comprehension levels.

Learning to read and reading to learn never stops—it goes on each day of the year, each year of our lives; so, too, must teaching to read and reading to teach—the challenge is not to criticise but to find better ways.[32]

Reading speed can be improved through the systematic practice of more effective reading habits. Once you are convinced of the gains of rapid reading, it is just a matter of breaking the accustomed tempo. You must practise faster reading on simple, narrative and interesting reading material. Gradually when you get used to faster reading, you develop confidence in yourself, then you can try to read relatively less simple material. In due course, you will find that you are able to read all kinds of material proportionately faster.

At the initial stages of practice, when you aim at reading faster than you normally read, it is obvious that you would feel as if you are having a different experience. It is just like your first experience of a flight or any other similar experience where innumerable imaginary fears stood in your way. In the same way, initially you may feel that in attempting to read faster, you may probably miss the message. In reality it is not so and there is nothing to get worried over it. It cannot happen because the reading material is so simple and there is nothing that can create any problem of understanding. Gradually with little more practice you will be able to understand better by faster reading. Have confidence in your abilities. You can definitely read faster. Try to have a thorough grasp of the process of reading and compare it with the way you read. Furthermore,

(*a*) Sharpen your speed of perception which relates to rapid word recognition skills,

(*b*) Enlarge your 'span of recognition' and try to read in thought units,

(*c*) Make an effort to minimise sub-vocalisation (if not altogether eliminate, because that will be an impossibility) or even vocalisation (if you are used to it),

(*d*) Avoid unnecessary regressions, read with concentration and attention,

(*e*) Maintain a regular record of your reading speed and each time try to beat your earlier speed,

(*f*) Build up a stamina for reading,

(*g*) Have a strong motivation and interest for reading, and above all, (*h*) Cultivate a desire to improve your existing reading speed with systematic and regular reading practice with a spirit of interest, willingness and competition within yourself.

SUMMARY

What a person reads is as important as how well he reads it. Inefficient reading habits come in the way of rapid reading and act as barriers to speed-reading. Faulty visual perception, word by word reading, regressions, finger pointing and head swinging, vocalisation, sub-vocalisation, lack of stamina, lack of motivation and reading interests are some of the barriers which come in the way of developing greater speed in reading. The other barriers are word blocking, word analysis, monotonous plodding, back-tracking, re-reading, readability, mode and purpose, and lack of concentration. Speed-reading practice is suitable only for those individuals whose word recognition, vocabulary and comprehension are already adequate. Deficiencies in any of these areas should be remedied before time pressures are imposed. Regular and systematic practice with very easy, highly interesting material, read for less exacting purposes, is a natural effective means of increasing reading speed.

REFERENCES

1. Jenkinson, Marion D. "Reading: A World Problem", in Marion D. Jenkinson (Ed.), *Reading Instruction: An International Forum,* Proceedings of the First World Congress on Reading held at UNESCO House, Paris, France, August 8-9, 1966, International Reading Association, Newark, Delaware, U.S.A., 1967, p. 17.
2. Anderson, Verna Dieckman. *Reading and Young Children,* The Macmillan Company, Toronto, Ontario, 1968 (Second Printing, 1969), pp. 5 and 354.
3. Anderson, Verna Dieckman. op. cit.
4. Heilman, Arthur W. *Improve Your Reading Ability,* Charles E. Merrill Books, Inc., Columbus, Ohio, 1962, pp. 115 and 6.
5. Heilman, Arthur W. op. cit.
6. Adams, W. Royce. *Increasing Reading Speed,* The Macmillan Company, Collier-Macmillan Limited, London, 1969 (Second Printing, 1970), pp. 43, 59 and 94.
7. Harris, Albert J. *How to Increase Reading Ability,* Fifth Edition, David McKay Company, Inc., New York, 1970 (Fifth Printing, 1974), pp. 497-98.
8. Kohl, Herbert. *Reading How to,* Penguin Education, 1974, pp. 119-120.

9. Harris, Albert J. op. cit.
10. Ahuja, G. C. "The Effect of Vocalisation on Reading Speed and Comprehension", *Teacher Education,* 9 (4), (July 1975), 20-23.
11. Fry, Edward B. *Reading Instruction for Classroom and Clinic,* McGraw Hill Book Company, New York, 1972, p. 432.
12. Lewis, Norman. *How to Read Better and Faster,* Third Edition, Thomas Y. Crowell Co., New York, 1958.
13. Fry, Edward. *Teaching Faster Reading—A Manual,* The University Press, Cambridge 1963, pp. 16-17.
14. Kohl, Herbert. *Reading How to,* Penguin Education, op. cit.
15. Smith, Henry P and Dechant, Emerald V. *Psychology in Teaching Reading,* Prentice-Hall International, Inc., London, 1961, p. 272.
16. Allport, Gorden W. *Personality A Psychological Interpretation,* Henry Holt and Company, New York, 1937, p. 201.
17. Getzels, Jacob W. "The Nature of Reading Interests: Psychological Aspects", *Developing Permanent Interest in Reading,* Supplementary Educational Monographs No, 84, University of Chicago Press, Chicago, 1956, p. 7.
18. Bond, Guy L and Tinker, Miles A. *Reading Difficulties: Their Diagnosis and Correction,* Second Edition Appleton-Century-Crofts, New York, 1967, pp. 448-49.
19. Eysenck, H J. *The Structure of Human Personality,* Methuen and Company, Ltd., London, 1953, p. 213.
20. Ryans, David G. "Motivation in Learning", in *Psychology of Learning,* Forty-first Yearbook of the National Society for the Study of Education, Part II, University of Chicago Press, Chicago, 1942, p. 312.
21. Smith, Henry P and Dechant, Emerald V. *Psychology in Tradining Reading,* op. cit.
22. James, William. *Principles of Psychology,* Vol 2, Henry Holt and Company, 1890, p. 111.
23. Witty, Paul. "Interest and Success—The Antidote to Stress", *Elementary English,* 32, (December 1955), 507-13.
24. Nemoitin, Bernard O. "Relation Between Interest and Achievement", *Journal of Applied Psychology,* 16 (1), (1932), 59-73.
25. Bernstein, Margery R. "Relationship Between Interest and Reading Comprehension", *Journal of Educational Research,* 49, (December 1955), 283-88.
26. Wheat, H. G. *Foundations of School Learning,* Alfred A. Knopf, New York, 1955, pp. 57-58.
27. Norvell, George W. "Some Results of a Twelve-Year Study of Children's Reading Interests", *English Journal,* 35, (December, 1946), 536.
28. Schnayer, Sidney W. "Some Relations Between Reading Interests and Reading Comprehension", *Doctoral Dissertation,* University of California at Berkeley, 1967.
29. Adams, W. Royce. op. cit.
30. Thomas, Ellen Lamar and Robinson, H. Alan. *Improving Reading in Every Class,* Abridged Edition, Allyn and Bacon, Inc., Boston, 1972, (Fourth Printing, July 1974), p. 137.
31. Adams, W. Royce. *Increasing Reading Speed,* op. cit.
32. Anderson, Verna Dickman. *Reading and Young Children,* op. cit.

4

THE ART OF RAPID READING

The value of the ability to read rapidly and efficiently is being realised by people in all walks of life. Rapid reading habits enable a person to get more in a comparatively lesser time which is the need of the hour. We are living a very busy life and hardly find any time to keep ourselves fully informed about what is going on around us. The possession of rapid reading ability comes to our rescue in our busy schedule. It helps us in enriching our life with plenty of materials from different areas, becoming more efficient in our professional undertaking and rendering greater service to mankind.

Have you ever thought of what per cent of your waking hours is expended within the boundary of printed symbols? Imagine a fine morning when you get up from your bed and your wife offers you a hot cup of tea. While taking that cup of tea from her hand you start reading her face and if you read some signs of annoyance, you can never dare ask for the second cup. Can you? After tea perhaps you have to go through the contents of a book which your child has brought to you as he wants you to tell him the answers to some of the questions. You may perhaps fear taking a long time in reading the book as otherwise your child may think that you are a slow reader. Next comes the newspaper and you have hardly the time to go through the whole of its contents because you have to finish your breakfast, etc., and then get ready for the office. While on your way to office you come across many posters on both sides of the road which you cannot avoid reading. After reaching your office, you find you have to go through a heap of files. Reading is again involved. So you cannot help it and the whole day goes on in reading many letters, documents, memoranda and what not!

Not only this, again when you reach home, though you are dead tired you feel the need for either reading a newspaper or a magazine or going through a novel or some other book. Still, your reading job does not end here. If you are a person who is professionally committed you would like to enrich yourself with the increasing knowledge so that you could remain abreast of the latest developments in your area of work. The problem is not of having more time, but how best to make use of the time that we have at our disposal. Here arises the need to learn and apply rapid reading techniques. It is then only that we would be able to complete our reading assignments much better and quicker.

Suppose a person has about 150 pages to read daily and that his reading rate is 150 words per minute. It would take at least 3 minutes (assuming that a page has 450 words) to read one page and about 7 hours and 30 minutes to read 150 pages. This will only be possible if a person does nothing else except keeps reading at a stretch. In actual practice, it may even take 9 hours or more.

On the contrary if he can read at a speed of 300 or even 450 words per minute which is quite possible, he would only take 3 hours and 45 minutes or even 2 hours and 30 minutes. A person can even go beyond the speed of 450 words per minute. Some fantastic readers can even reach the ceiling which is around 900 words per minute. A person can skim about four to six times faster than he reads. This very clearly means that if he can employ this technique for some of the materials for which he does not need minute details, he can save plenty of his time. All reading materials do not require equal attention. Some can surely be read much faster such as newspapers, popular magazine articles, etc. If we apply slow and careful reading techniques for each and everything that we read, it will be a colossal waste of time. A good reader is always a shrewd discriminator. He makes an intelligent decision as to how fast he should go ahead.

Comprehension and not the speed should be our prime consideration, but nothing much is achieved in brooding over the same material the whole day to get a thorough comprehension. Fast readers may not in all cases be good comprehenders but poor readers are necessarily poor comprehenders. Research evidence shows[1] that fast readers make good comprehenders.

Fast readers and slow readers may or may not comprehend well, and sometimes the fast reader comprehends better than the slow reader. This happens when the fast reader is reading approximately as rapidly as his comprehension abilities allow and when the slow reader is reading more slowly than his comprehension permits, he is in effect allowing time to his mind to wander from the task.[2]

Reading at a very rapid rate is of little value if we understand very little of what we have read. On the other hand reading with a high degree of comprehension without caring much about the time spent in reading will be equally of little use.

A study[3] revealed that the silent reading speed of seventh standard pupils (when they were given very easy and interesting reading material) was 179 words per minute.

In the Central Institute of Indian Languages, Mysore, we conducted Rapid Reading Courses for different categories of officers. The silent reading speed for each of the groups was checked before each course began. This was done individually by making each participant read simple and interesting narrative material. The silent reading speeds of three different groups[4,5,6] were found to be 212, 209 and 227 words per minute respectively.

It is interesting to note that there was a marginal difference in the reading rates of the seventh standard pupils and highly educated mature adults when both the groups were given simple and interesting narrative material to read. This obviously is a matter of great concern.

Buswell[7] has had, in his college classes, students of unquestioned intelligence who were slow, clumsy readers because their basic reading ability was permitted to level off too soon. On tests of basic reading they scored below sixth-grade norms.

The speaker who is too slow not only loses track of the matter, he also harms the listener. Some people report that when they have to listen to very slow speakers, they very soon get headaches and cannot enjoy the contents of the speech. Keeping in view physiological speech limits, we do not recommend a fantastically speedy speech but extremely slow speech is also of no use. Similar is the case with reading. Too fantastic a reading speed crossing physiological perceptual limits is of no use because it impedes comprehension. Too slow a reading is altogether hopeless since it does not help in comprehension. There is no support in research for the popular notion that slow reading leads to better comprehension.

Psychologically, the two processes that is, listening and reading are almost similar. However, the difference between the two is mainly in the sense avenues through which the verbal stimuli are sent to the brain. Ear has to serve as an active agent for the listening activity whereas eye does the reading business. Both the processes aim at just one focus and that is 'comprehension' which involves interpretation of the stimuli.

For listening no doubt the person has only to depend on his ears but it is the speaker who holds the privileged position. It is in his hands to control the speed. In spite of the fact that sometimes the listener is ready to listen in a speedy manner, he is not able to do so because the speaker is going slowly. Few people can talk intelligibly much faster than 200 words per minute. On the contrary reading can be much faster as it is a personal skill and one can go as fast as his limits permit keeping in view the purpose of reading at hand.

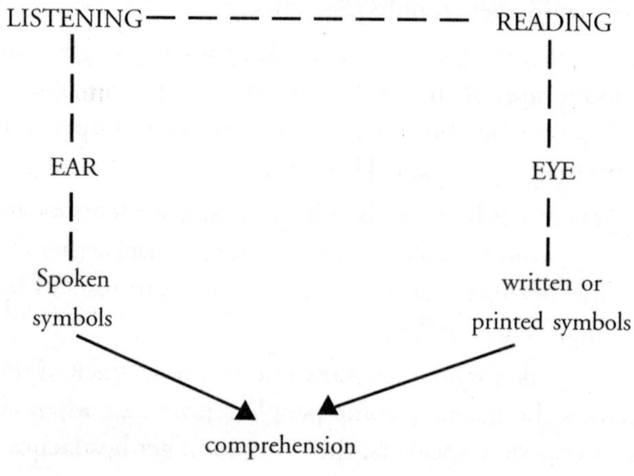

There are people who are voracious readers—they can read at fantastic speeds. Really speaking, reading is a skill which readily responds to practice. Continuous and systematic practice results in rate improvement.

Studies[8] in the area of reading speed and comprehension indicate that the rate of reading may be forced from 100 to 300 words per minute above the reader's present rate without a break in the level of tested comprehension.

Slow reading is not always bad. If you are reading material which involves following directions and your purpose is to achieve cent per cent comprehension, you must go very carefully so that even the minute details are thoroughly grasped. At certain moments slowness reflects beauty. It affords one the opportunity to evaluate, to criticise, to linger, to enjoy the beauty of a description and to read beyond the lines. But if one gets used to a slow pace and reads everything slowly, cautiously and carefully, then that also is no good. All reading materials do not require the same kind of attention and care.

If a person reads very slowly, word by word, he will be classified as an inefficient reader even though he may do well on comprehension. If on the other hand he is the most rapid reader on record but does not comprehend what he reads, he will be designated as a very poor or inefficient reader. The statement is often made that rapid readers also have superior comprehension of what they read. This has been stated or written in such a way that many people have generalised that rapid reading "causes" improved comprehension. It is more likely that rapid readers as a group are highly skilled in all facets of reading and are simply highly efficient readers. They are probably more flexible readers, read more widely and have a wider background or reading interests than do slower readers.[9]

Singleton[10] writes as follows:

"The reader needs to know the vocabulary of the field he chooses to read. I consider myself a skilled reader but I can't read my wife's knitting directions. The first lines usually read: cast on 88 stitches; knit two, purl two, for a total of 90 rows. Now, I know every word in those directions but I can't follow them. My concepts of cast, knit, and purl are not sufficiently well developed. My inclination is to cast directions, yarn, and needles across the room ... A dictionary definition of purl is not sufficient for me to know how to purl. I must be shown how and I must practice it until I become a purler. This would be a normally expected outcome of a course in knitting.

"Likewise, a complete understanding of words like map, meridian, plateau, capital and range is a normally expected outcome of instruction in geography."

The best foundation for learning to read faster, therefore, consists of adequate knowledge of vocabulary and good comprehension.

The essence of speed-reading is a good full mind, which understands relationships, handles language with great facility, and a personality which yearns and needs to collect information.[11]

An Efficient Reader Is a Flexible Reader

We daily need to read plenty of materials in the form of newspapers, journals, reports, correspondence, memoranda and books. It is not essential that we should follow the same reading speeds for all types of reading and if we do, more man-hours will be consumed which is again an expensive affair. It appears to be very much wasteful for not everything requires the same amount of attention and concentration. Fast reading habits therefore, are of great value to any reader. With our rapidly expanding field of human knowledge, demands are being made to read more and more in less and less time. The benefits of reading faster can never be underestimated. To be able to read more in a comparatively lesser time can be a great blessing. To enjoy reading extensively, one must be a proficient reader.

The efficient, skilful reader can move with a kind of relentless concentration through a veritable mountain of material at speeds which to the plodding reader seem fantastic. In effect, the disciplined reader blots out distractions and, almost like a machine, cuts through a pile of materials. If you watch him closely, you will see that he scans, skips, skims, stops, and reads closely as his interests and the relevance or importance of the materials dictate. He has become the effective user of a valuable, high-powered reading tool.[12]

Carrillo and Sheldon[13] have suggested that the ability to read rapidly is a prerequisite to reading flexibly. Several tests of reading flexibility have been developed, including those of Letson[14] and Braam and Sheldon.[15] New developments in testing flexibility are discussed by Ironside,[16] who compares various tests with criteria suggested by Carrillo and Sheldon.[17] Regarding testing for flexibility, Berg[18] concludes that flexibility in reading is the product of an attitude and environment that offers the reader a maximum of psychological freedom and safety.

Flexibility in reading rates is the skill of not reading everything in the same manner. Flexibility enables a reader to vary his reading rate according to the nature of materials to be read. Flexibility in reading rate is a sign of maturity. It is anti-rigidity. It shows a dynamic approach to reading speed. Flexibility involves separating wheat from the chaff. It is adaptability. A flexible reader is always an adaptable reader. At the very first sight of the reading materials he is able to decide his destination and the different conveyances which he will be using to reach that destination.

A very common weakness found among almost many adult readers is the habit of reading practically all materials at the same uniform speed. This is utter waste of time because each and every piece of reading material does not demand the same speed. A relatively large portion of the daily newspapers, popular magazines, fiction and feature articles can be read faster than the average textbook or scientific or literary works. A flexible reader has several reading speeds at his disposal which he can use according to the nature of the reading task at hand. Even with one reading task, he uses several reading speeds. He knows that a number of words in any given passage could be ignored in reading without destroying the meaning. Moreover each word or each phrase in a given passage does not have equal weight as far as helping the reader arrive at the main idea contained in that passage is concerned.

The key word for successful flexibility is comprehension. The reader should be able to identify the level of comprehension necessary for successful reading to take place. Once he has settled on the level of comprehension, then he can adjust his rate. Optimum reading flexibility is the condition that exists when the reader can accomplish his reading task with a minimum amount of time and the least expenditure of physiological and psychological effort. Therefore, the two primary questions a flexible reader should ask are: (1) How much time do I have? and (2) What type of comprehension is necessary? Once he has answered these questions he is in a position to select his reading rate.[19]

Jack Holmes[20] states as follows:

"The secret of good reading lies in the ability to know when and how to change pace. The mundane material concerning the commerce of life may well be read quickly; but when one comes to the crux of the message, or when one fortuitously encounters one of those fountainhead concepts from which idea flow, then one must deliberately drink the delightful draught until the full meaning has been drained. Even then such passages are well-springs that may be read again, each time affording the reader a little deeper insight, a greater understanding, a new zest for life!

"Indeed, the deepest satisfactions come not when one is able to read a book in 30 minutes flat (the goal stressed by some teachers today), but rather when one chances upon a beautifully written passage carrying so much meaning, sparkle, and conviction that it verily sings—as when great poetry clarifies the meaning of life and causes one to bring his value system into closer harmony with the realities of the universe.

"As one pushes his speed above the four to eight 'hundred' words per minute mark into the next higher order of magnitude, say two to eight 'thousand' words per minute, the reader simply rides in on the crest of the wave. As his eyes race down the page, it is true that he may learn to catch the gist of the story; but the beauty of the syntax, the style, the sting, the twinkle, the music in the well-turned phrase, the technical explanation, or logic of a philosophical discussion cannot be truly pondered, grasped, and appreciated."

Agnella Gunn[21] writes:

"How fast do you read the instructions for a Do It Yourself project? Recently the writer received a great, flat carton in which was packed an unassembled picnic table and benches, complete with mimeographed instructions for assembling. Weekend house guests included three teachers who had taught or were teaching reading. All of us took turns reading, more importantly, interpreting, and still more importantly applying the message. Did we read slowly? We did indeed! We not only read slowly, we stopped, checked, and then re-read. Then we read aloud. We discussed. Yes we argued. We pointed with our fingers to what we were reading. Were we unmotivated readers? Disinterested? Handicapped? Not on your life! But the going was tough. The reading traffic was heavy; the instructions were compressed and the procedures, strange; the vocabulary was unfamiliar. Our combined reading rates would probably have gone off the wrong end of the graph. But our reading was efficient. Our comprehension was high. Our interpretation and application were faultless. Our mission was accomplished (you should see our garden equipment). But rapid rate? No. That we did not have.

"On the other hand, contrast such a task in reading with that presented by some of today's light fiction—you pick the title. You can read with the TV on full blast; you can listen for the telephone; you can eat; you can hear the sprinkler system on the lawn or the folks in the next apartment; you can tease your dog with your foot; you can even carry on a kind of desultory conversation without being distracted or losing anything of the familiar yet predictable details, the expected facts, the sometimes clever but rarely disturbing situations, or the obvious, seldom varying sentence sequences. It is easy, trivial reading. It may be relaxing reading. It may even be interesting reading, but it is impoverished literature. The traffic in ideas is light; the reading road, open; the material and language are familiar. Such printed matter provides evidence of what reading at its best has to offer. You can zoom through it as rapidly as you wish, may be as fast as you can flip the pages—until you are wakened by the book slipping out of your hands.

"High variable reading rates are something like money in the bank. You can hardly have too much but you need to learn to use both money and speed wisely."

An efficient reader reads well whether he is reading literature, geography, science or business management. The reader who reads well gets at the heart of the material, understands it, organises it, assimilates it, criticises it and elaborates upon it. He purposely puts himself in the attitude-set of the author and reads with slow or rapid speed or moderate speed, according to the material he is reading.

Singleton[22] writes as follows:

"The point is, reading is reading, but *for what?* The *for what* is the key. The skilled reader knows his purpose in reading. Whether we call this purposeful reading, or variable speed-reading, adapting one's reading to the purpose for which one is reading makes little difference. It is not how we call it but what we do. Reading instruction should include plenty of practice in different reading attacks according to the purpose for which one is reading.

"Varying reading attack to suit the material to be read is the name of the game. A reader who varies habitually is well fitted to read in any of the content areas. The only additional skill he needs is knowledge of the content area itself."

Harlan J. Shores[23] writes:

"To ask how rapidly a person should read or what he should comprehend is useless. These questions would never be asked by anyone with even an elementary understanding of the nature of the reading process. Neither speed nor comprehension goals are meaningful apart from specific materials or apart from the purposes for which they are read. People read some materials rapidly for some purposes. The same people read other materials, or the same materials, slowly for different purposes. People comprehend some materials easily for some purposes and other materials, or even the same materials, poorly for other purposes.

"Flexibility is the ability to adjust reading skills to varied materials and purposes for reading. It may be important to note at this point that the flexible reader is not necess .rily the good reader any more than the rapid reader is necessarily t.ıє good reader. One cannot be a good reader without being a flexible ɾeader, but one can be a flexible reader without being a good reader. If a reader had all the reading and thinking skills at his command, if he knew how and when to use each singly and in combination, he would be both a flexible reader and a good reader. Lacking as we all are in both thinking and reading skills, we attack the problem on three fronts. We learn to think more adequately. We develop our reading skills, and especially those necessary for different materials and different purposes. And we become more flexible in choosing the best skills and abilities for the reading job at hand."

Agnella Gunn[24] suggests:

"The affective connotation of speed is a favourable one. Fast is good. So, of course, slow is bad. But slow reading is not necessarily bad. Nor is fast reading necessarily good. Reading rate is a minor element in the total operation; by itself it is almost meaningless. It is rather like rate of speed in driving a car. Any given speed can be either too slow or too fast depending upon the circumstances.

In reading, is rapid rate good?

Yes, with some types of materials.

Yes, in certain situations.

Yes, for some purposes.

Yes, up to a point.

"Yes, when built on the basic reading skills which support it. But reading slowly is not the answer either. Some read slowly with poor results; others read rapidly with no better results. The reading rate itself is not important, but what goes on in the reader's head at a certain rate is vitally important."

Adams[25] writes:

"Not long ago a study was made of the reading potential of 1500 Harvard and Radcliffe freshman students. They were assigned a thirty-page chapter of detailed material in a history book and told only to study the chapter for a test which would require answering multiple choice questions and writing a short essay. After twenty-two minutes, the students were stopped and asked to report on their method of approach. More than 90 per cent reported that they started at the beginning of the chapter and read straight through. When tested on the material they had covered, all did well on the multiple choice questions. But when it came to writing a short statement about what the chapter covered, only 15 out of 1500 could do it. Yet, the end of the reading selection contained a section headed "Recapitulation" with a summary of the entire chapter on which the students were being tested. If the readers had focused on the entire chapter before reading it quickly, they would have had enough information to help them write a short statement on the chapter's content.

"The report reflects a major problem with readers, particularly students. They have the idea that a slow careful reading, beginning with page 1 and plodding along to the end, is the best way to read most things. While it may work well for very difficult, unfamiliar material, it is not necessarily the way to read closely."

The competent reader must constantly vary his procedures. Now he skims over several pages for a overview based on sentences in bold type and on charts and diagrams; now he reads a paragraph slowly because it describes an idea difficult to grasp; now he scoots through another paragraph which states supplementary matter that he does not wish to study at the moment; now he turns back a page or two to check the relation of an idea there with one he has just read; and now he looks away from the page for a moment to chew upon the ideas that have piled up in his mind.[26]

Speed Signals

The following speed signals suggested by Thomas and Robinson[27] will serve as guidelines for an efficient reader:

(1)Reduce Speed Signals

- Unfamiliar terms.
- Difficult sentence or paragraph structure.
- Difficult concepts.
- Detailed technical materials – especially those on which you have scant background.
- Difficult and detailed directions.
- Material on which you want detailed retention.

- Material with a diagram, requiring constant shifting from text to diagram.
- Material you wish to weigh carefully.
- Material that requires "visualising time".
- Artistic writing which invites your lingering.

(2) Increase Speed Signals

- Simple materials with few ideas new to you.
- Examples and illustrations unnecessary for understanding.
- Detailed explanation and elaboration which you do not need.
- Ideas which are restatements of previous ones.
- Material from which you want only the more important ideas and facts.

Angella Gunn[28] writes:

"Our advice to readers should be something like this: Reading speed is—or should be—a variable. On a clear, open highway with nothing to challenge you, nothing memorable to cling to your mind, speed right ahead. But with heavy traffic of demanding ideas—slow down. Even draw off to the side and stop completely to consider, compare, contrast, evaluate, absorb.

"Emphasis on increasing speed unquestionably is desirable—if it contributes to the development of readers who not only read rapidly but, more importantly, who read flexibly, accurately, critically."

Characteristics of Good and Poor Readers

Some of the characteristics which sharply differentiate between good and poor readers have been enumerated below.

Good Reader

1. Rich vocabulary
2. Reads in larger thought units or phrases
3. Makes only needed fixations as the material demands
4. Wider span of recognition

5. Takes very little time for each fixation
6. Rhythmic return sweeps
7. Total or near total absence of vocalisation
8. Always makes use of greater contextual constraints
9. Perfect eye-mind co-ordination
10. Reads with confidence
11. Reads with a definite purpose
12. Can read even beyond the lines
13. Smooth and effective reading
14. Positive and lively attitude
15. A wide variety of reading interests
16. Mostly alert while reading
17. No retention problems
18. Uses several speeds
19. Has the experience of wide, extensive reading
20. Has a pragmatic outlook about the difficulty level of the material
21. A very strong stamina
22. Possesses a high level of motivation
23. Has no concentration problems
24. Changes his speed and even reading technique according to the nature of the reading material
25. Reading is always a spontaneous, light and pleasant activity. He can find something satisfying and enjoyable in every kind of reading material.

Poor Reader

1. Poor vocabulary
2. Reads word by word
3. Makes more fixations
4. Very narrow span of recognition

5. Duration of fixation is long
6. Return sweeps are irregular
7. Excessive vocalisation
8. Does not take help from contextual clues
9. Eye-mind co-ordination is sometimes lacking
10. Lacks confidence
11. Reads without a clear purpose
12. Cannot reach the critical level of reading
13. Reading speed is hindered by back-tracking, re-focusing or re-reading
14. Neutral or even negative attitude towards reading
15. Reading interests are very limited
16. Daydreams very freely
17. Has poor retention
18. Has only one speed
19. Has a very poor reading background
20. Overestimates the difficulty of the material
21. No stamina for reading
22. Lacks motivation
23. Poor concentration
24. Reads all types of materials with extra care as if it were a legal document
25. Takes reading as a tiresome activity.

How Fast Should You Read? It Depends

How fast you can read depends, then, on what you are reading, why you are reading it, and how much you already know about the subject. You can "speed-read" a Shakespearean sonnet, but will you really understand it? That would be like "speed hearing" a Beethoven symphony. You can read slowly, word by word, a front page newspaper article, but is it necessary for total comprehension? A good reader concerns himself less with speed itself and more with his purpose for reading.[29]

The good, rapid reader does not of course, read equally fast everything he reads. To be sure, he may read everything proportionately faster than a slow reader, but certainly on occasion, he does take things slowly. It is the ability to adapt rate to the requirements of reading task that is of the greatest importance. The slow reader cannot do this. Fast readers as a group certainly learn as much from a single reading as do slow readers. It takes considerable practice to make one a flexible reader—sometimes reading at top speeds and other times slowing down to the maximum. The important point is—it is not difficult; it can be done.

There is always a possibility that some individuals will fall so much in love with speed-reading that they will start thinking 'speed-reading' as an end in itself rather than as a skill which can be used in some reading situations. An efficient reader regards speed of reading as a mere convenience for doing more reading rather than as an end in itself. An efficient reader has several reading speeds at his disposal and he is able to adjust his reading speed to the purposes for which he reads keeping in view the very nature of the reading materials. He is satisfied to read some materials with the speed of wind, others with a very slow speed giving deliberate attention to minor details in the form of different sentences, phrases and even words without worrying much about the time consumed.

An efficient reader is a rapid, economical, flexible, voracious, critical, versatile, proficient and above all an interested reader.

SUMMARY

With our rapidly expanding field of human knowledge, demands are being made to read more and more in less and less time. The art of efficient reading comes to our rescue in today's busy life. The benefits of reading faster are incalculable. It is not essential that we should follow the same reading speed for all types of reading and if we do, more man-hours will be consumed which is again an expensive affair. An efficient reader is always a flexible reader. When an efficient reader reduces his speed, he does so for a purpose. He reduces his speed because the materials require him to think more slowly. The efficient reader seeks to increase his understanding without sacrificing speed unnecessarily, or sometimes he may want to increase his speed without sacrificing his understanding. The flexible reader gears his reading rate to his thinking rate. Reading efficiency characterised with flexibility is an asset to any reader. To enjoy reading extensively, one must be a proficient reader.

REFERENCES

1. Ahuja, G. C. "Do Fast Readers Comprehend Better", *Journal of Educational Research and Extension,* 12 (2), (October 1975), 71-75.
2. Dechant, Emerald. *Reading Improvement in the Secondary School,* Prentice-Hall, Inc., Englewood Cliffs, New Jersey, 1973, p. 318.
3. Ahuja, Pramila and Ahuja, G. C. "Assessment of Silent Versus Oral Reading Speed and Comprehension of School Children", Research Abstract, *Journal of Education and Psychology,* 33 (2), (July 1975), 45-51.
4. Report of the Rapid Reading Course for the Commissioned Officers of the Indian Navy held at the Central Institute of Indian Languages, Mysore from 7th to 21st April, 1975.
5. Report of the Rapid Reading Course for the Senior Executives of the State Bank of India conducted by Central Institute of Indian Languages, Mysore at State Bank Staff College, Hyderabad from 15th to 29th December, 1975.
6. Report of the Second Rapid Reading Course for the Senior Executives of the State Bank of India conducted by the Central Institute of Indian Languages, Mysore at State Bank Staff College, Hyderabad from 17th to 22nd May, 1976.
7. Buswell, Guy T. "The Process of Reading", in Wilma H. Miller., *Elementary Reading Today,* Holt, Rinehart and Winston, Inc., New York, 1972, pp. 5-6.
8. Buswell, Guy T. "The Process of Reading" *Vistas in Reading,* ... op. cit.
9. Heilman, Arthur W. *Improve Your Reading Ability,* Charles E. Merrill Books, Inc., Columbus, Ohio, 1962, p. 8.
10. Singleton, Carlton M in Nila Banton Smith, (ed.), *Current Issues in Reading,* ibid., pp. 40-41.
11. Howards, Melvin. "Strategies for Improving our Concepts and Techniques in Regard to Speeds in Reading", Abstracts, *Fifteenth Annual Convention,* International Reading Association, Newark, Delaware, 1970, p. 42.
12. Gunn, Agnella M in Nila Banton Smith, (ed.), *Current Issues in Reading,* Vol. 13, Part 2, Proceedings of the Thirteenth Annual Convention, International Reading Association, Newark, Delaware 1971, 1969 (Third Printing, November 1970), pp. 79-84.
13. Carrillo, Lawrence and Sheldon, William D. "Flexibility of Reading Rate", *Journal of Educational Psychology,* 43, (May 1952), 299-305.
14. Letson, Charles T. "The Construction and Evaluation of a Test to Measure the Flexibility of Reading Rate", *Doctoral Dissertation,* Boston University School of Education, 1956.

15. Braam, Leonard S and Sheldon, William D. *Developing Efficient Reading,* Oxford University Press, New York, 1959.

16. Ironside, Roderick A. "New Development in the Reading Test: Testing Rate Flexibility", *Proceedings of College Reading Association,* 4, (September 1963) 26-30.

17. Carrillo, Lawrence and Sheldon, William D. *Flexibility of Rates, Journal of Educational Psychology,* 43, ... op. cit.

18. Berg, Paul Conard. "Flexibility in Reading", *Vistas in Reading,* Proceedings of the International Reading Association, Vol. 2, Part 1, 1966 (copyright 1967), 45-48.

19. Nason, Harold M and McDonald, Arthur S. "Reading Flexibility" *Reading in High School,* 1 (3), (1964).

20. Holmes, Jack A. "Speed, Comprehension and Power in Reading", in Lawrence E Hafner., *Improving Reading in Secondary Schools,* Selected Readings, The Macmillan Company, New York, 1967, p. 65.

21. Gunn, Agnella M in Nila Banton Smith, (ed.), *Current Issues in Reading,* ... op. cit.

22. Singleton, Carlton M in Nila Banton Smith, (ed.), *Current Issues in Reading,* ... op. cit.

23. Shores, J. Harlan. "Developing purposeful and Flexible Reading in Grades Four Through Eight", in Larry A. Harris and Carl B. Smith, *Individualising Reading Instruction—A Reader,* Holt, Rinehart and Winston, Inc., New York, 1972, p. 303.

24. Gunn, Agnella M in Nila Banton Smith, (ed.), *Current issues in Reading* ... op. cit.

25. Adams, W. Royce. *Increasing Reading Speed,* The Macmillan Company, Collier-Macmillan Limited, London, 1969 (Second Printing, 1970), p. 21.

26. Shaw, Phillip. "Achieving Personal Maturity Through Reading and by Recognizing and Constructing Meaning", in Mildred A. Dawson, (Compiler), *Developing Comprehension Including Critical Reading,* International Reading Association, Newark, Delaware, 1968, p. 55.

27. Thomas, Ellen Lamar and Robinson, H. Alan. *Improving Reading in Every Class,* Abridged Edition, Allyn and Bacon, Inc., Boston, 1972 (Fourth Printing, July 1974), p. 147.

28. Gunn, Agnella M in Nila Banton Smith, (ed.), *Current Issues in Reading* .... op. cit.

29. Adams, W. Royce. *Increasing Reading Speed,* The Macmillan Company Limited, London, op. cit.

5

SKIMMING AND SCANNING

Efficient readers do not always aspire for maximum comprehension. If they did they would not be able to read much and their experiences would remain very limited. They are bound to follow a flexible approach going from fantastic speeds to slow, careful speeds with a clear purpose in mind. There are fastest speeds which are used in skimming and scanning and also slow and careful reading speeds which are used while reading critically for integrated study purposes.

Skimming is a reading skill which demands topmost speeds. It is a method of quickly gathering information from the printed page. In skimming, you allow your eyes to travel over a page very quickly, stopping only here and there to gain an idea.

For the most part, skimming involves skill in skipping the irrelevant parts and judiciously selecting those that are relevant. The greater the background or familiarity in a field, the greater the facility in skimming. Most decidedly, skimming is an active process. It is guided by a definite purpose. The reader employs his own experience and information from other sources to check the relevance and accuracy of new acquisitions.[1]

Finally, skimming is a specific type of reading. Appreciation, seeing relationships, studying context and other critical-reading skills are minimised. Speed is emphasised. The eye skims through the material without the reader's resorting to vocalisation or even sub-vocalisation. The mind is alerted by a specific cue or cues, thereby grasping a minimum of content. The mental process involved in recognising these cues causes the reader to change pace when necessary and thus to absorb only the desired information. Learning to skim is a very valuable academic exercise.

How to Skim

Tinker and McCullough[2] give the following procedures as samples:

(*a*) Examining the preface, table of contents, and section headings in chapters of a book to note what is included, or to judge whether it is likely to contain the information you are seeking.

(*b*) Sampling various pages in a story or novel to decide whether it is easy enough to read, or if it seems to you to be worth reading.

(*c*) Sampling the introduction, topic sentences of paragraphs and conclusions of a controversial article to get the author's point of view.

(*d*) Examination of the introduction, section headings, illustrations or maps, and conclusions of a chapter to get the framework on which the topic is developed.

(*e*) Examination of headlines, accompanying illustrations, and perhaps topic sentences in introductory paragraphs of newspaper articles to decide whether you wish to read the article. This procedure can be a great time saver for the reader.

Are There Many Types

Schale[3] discusses three techniques, all involving skimming, for increasing rate of reading by learning to read vertically: the vertical skimming method, the square span method, and the narrow column method.

In the vertical skimming method, the reader may glide his eyes over the irrelevant content until he lands on what he is looking for (exclusive skimming); he may survey material, identifying main ideas and inferring less important details (inclusive skimming); or he may, using non-directed skimming move his eyes down the page in a narrow span. The square span method and the narrow column metho ¹ both involve moving the eye over a small span—either the eye focuses on the centre of a page or all the words are placed in narrow columns. Less skimming is involved in the latter two approaches.

Too frequently the ability to skim is not well learned. Grayum[4] studied this ability in six groups ranging from fourth graders to college students and well read adults. The intelligence and reading ability of everyone in the groups were average or above. The results revealed marked differences among the individuals at each of the grade levels in the ability to skim. Some readers, both average and superior, were very poor in skimming. In fact some adults were skimming as poorly as some fourth graders.

One hears reports of people who profess to be able to read in excess of 4000 words per minute, but this tremendous rate is based on a skimming technique to obtain the gist of a passage rather than a full reading of the passage and is probably obtained by reading vertically rather than from left to right. At an advanced stage such a technique where the eye is fixed upon the centre of the line and thus takes in a word or two on either side of this point can be an advantage but it is unsuitable for children. The reader moves the eye from line to line, from the top to the bottom of the page ignoring the words at either end of each line.[5]

Skimming usually takes the form of preview, overview, or review.[6] In skimming for overview purposes the reader gets a general impression of the content. He reads more of the material than when doing preview skimming. He looks for the writer's organisation, thinks along with the writer, and notes the transitions. Skimming for review is a useful technique in preparing for tests or to increase retention generally.

When should the pupil be taught to skim? Taylor and Frackenpohl[7] have identified the type of pupil who is ready for selective reading. The pupil must be a flexible reader. He needs visual co-ordination. He must have developed a proper directional attack, and must be able to organise a series of data. He must be able to identify words rapidly, he must relate them to each other. He must develop attention and concentration, while maintaining his composure. He must be relaxed and willing to settle for less than complete comprehension.

The pupil must develop a new perceptual skill. In selective reading "looking" is as important as reading. The person must look back and forth and down the page in a floating manner as it were.[8] He learns to take in words, ideas, and organisation at a subliminal level.

Breaking the Accustomed Tempo

Normally, our eyes move from left to right across the page, and for this reason all of us are accustomed to using our 'lateral' field of vision. We fixate at a point on a line and read all the other words we can see at the left and right of this fixation, then move on to another fixation and repeat the perception process. But it happens that we also possess a vertical field of vision which usually lies dormant in so far as reading is concerned. It is possible to cultivate this to take words above and below the point of fixation, as well as at the left and right of it. Undoubtedly the phenomenal skimmers who claim they can grasp 3000 or 4000 words per minute make use of their vertical field of vision.[9]

Skimming demands fast moving of eyes down a page in a zigzag manner, looking for some words or phrases or sentences here and there to get the kernel of the material. Here, the eyes have to follow a pattern of seeing back and forth, down the page transporting bits of information or snatches of the messages to the mind as fast as possible. Making use of the index finger of the right hand when seeing back and forth down the page will facilitate faster processing.

Smith[10] writes:

"While skimming is the most useful of the reading skills, it is also the most complex. Skimming is a hierarchy built upon and utilising all other reading skills. In skimming you need to force your speed, to accelerate your reading tempo far beyond that used in your fastest reading of even easy material. In skimming you really 'fly' over the pages, but you should learn effective procedures for getting what you want while 'flying', or the flight will be a wasted effort.

"The swallow skims swiftly through the air catching and devouring insects while simultaneously flapping his wings to propel his body. He even drinks as he skims along over brooks, ponds and rivers, gathering drops of water in his beak with no cessation in flight.

This versatile creature does not pause or labour over any one insect or any one pool.

"The swallow's mode of skimming for food and water may be likened to the method used by skilled readers who skim over the pages of the print, gathering what they want as they 'fly' along. With instruction and practice a reader can become extremely adept in 'catching' what he desires from reading while 'on the wing'. This is the type of reading in which some people cover 3,000 or 4,000 words per minute and are able to repeat the gist of what they have read. They do not really read all of these words. It would be a physical impossibility for the eye to see that many words per minute. These people simply skim and pick up important snatches of content as they do so."

You should use a new pattern of eye movements—the pattern in which you sweep your eyes from the top to the bottom of pages. Let us say you have already developed excellent speed in reading horizontally from left to right. The next step is to develop skill in making fleeting eye sweeps vertically. The old habit of reading from left to right has been ingrained in your nervous system since childhood, and it may be difficult to develop vertical eye movements to a point at which they are as facile and fleeting as your horizontal eye movements.

Let us not forget that:

(*a*) Skimming is reading at the fastest speed which a person can accomplish.

(*b*) It is used when a reader wishes to cover material in a hurry.

(*c*) It is used when high comprehension is not required.

(*d*) It can be 4 to 6 times faster than your average reading speed.

As consideration is given to the very top levels of reading skill some misconceptions or misunderstandings may occur as to their nature and possibilities. Maximum rate of reading is one such example. Sometimes it is stated that a person can learn to read at a thousand or more words per minute; in such an instance, however, he would be 'skimming', not doing straight reading.[11] Although skimming is a useful skill, it should not be confused with straight reading.[12-13] Thus walking and running are useful, but different skills for which the record speeds per mile are about six and four minutes respectively. It would not be efficient to try to increase speed of walking by practising running.

Which method should be followed for skimming? In answer to this question, Gainsburg[14] writes:

"There is no exact method. Usually you concentrate on the longer words and skip many simple and common words that you meet in all your reading. You soon learn to pick words that seem to carry the ideas in the selection, and your mind fills in enough to permit you to skim ahead in the same way. You should actually read only about three or four words on a line, sometimes only two, sometimes as many as five."[15]

Scanning

Teachers and librarians often note students plodding line by line down a long column or page when all they actually want is a single bit of information. These students are surprised to learn that the date of an event, for example, can be located without reading every word—that, with practice, they can search out a given fact or figure from 15,000 or 20,000 words in a minute or two.[16]

Thomas and Robinson[17] present three levels of scanning: Level I scanning for a bit of information that stands out easily—the date of a historic discovery in science, or the university with which a noted author was affiliated. Level 2 scanning for an answer that is worded like the question. Level 3 scanning for an answer that is worded differently from a question.

Spache and Spache[18] identified three steps in the process of scanning:

(*a*) The student should fix in mind exactly what he is searching for. When possible, he should fix in mind the form in which the information is likely to appear.

(*b*) He should glance swiftly down the page or column expecting the information to stand out from the rest of the page.

(*c*) He should verify that he has indeed found the sought-for information (or else reject it) by reading carefully.

Thomas and Robinson[19] remark:

"Alerting students to conspicuous signposts of the author can markedly increase their speed in scanning. These include chapter titles, headings of chapter divisions, side headings close to the margin, and boldface or italic section headings. These signposts suggest whether the section at hand may yield the student what he is seeking or whether he can speed on past that section. Within a section, topic or concluding sentences sometimes suggest whether a certain paragraph is a promising or an unpromising hunting ground. By noting the author's signals the students can often rapidly bypass whole sections or chapters. Use of the index is another shortcut in scanning."

To have the ability to read at fantastic rates when the occasion demands has value, but nothing worthwhile can be gained unless we are able to comprehend at these speeds.

Skimming and Scanning Differentiated

Skimming and scanning are the two valuable techniques which can help the reader to read faster. Skimming is a rapid reading technique wherein the eye of the reader keeps floating over the reading material and scanning is a technique to find the facts in a very fast manner.

Skimming is quickly reading topic sentences but skipping over large sections of material. It is a sort of reading that is used to survey a selection, to get an overall picture of its holdings. This is the first stage for scanning. Scanning becomes easier if the skimming activity has been performed earlier.

Skimming differs from scanning in that the reader is not looking for the answer to a specific question. In fact, he may not have any definite idea of what he seeks, for example, when we take an unfamiliar book from the library to find out what it is about, we skim it by leafing through rapidly, glancing at the chapter titles, perhaps reading a few lines here and there. Sometimes while standing near the bookshelf itself we may skim the whole chapter which captivates us.

What do we do when we are scanning? This may be stated as follows:

(*a*) We move our eyes across the page as rapidly as possible to find the answer to a question.

(*b*) We must know exactly what we want to find before we begin to scan. We scan a crowd to find a certain person; we scan a heap of coconuts for finding a coconut of our choice; we scan over a box of tools for a hammer. In reading, we scan to find an answer to a particular question, to locate a specific date or number, or to locate a reference, a name, a city, or a quotation. And also, finding a particular phone number from the directory is a scanning activity.

Efficient scanning requires the reader to become aware of the importance of chapter titles, headings and sub-headings, the use of table of contents and the index. It should be understood that scanning is a speed technique that does not require reading of each and every word.

Thomas and Robinson[20] write:

"You will often need to use a book to search out a single fact, the answer to a single question, or one aspect of your topic. High speed scanning can 'save your time' in study. You learn to crack the printed page, moving your eyes down the page swiftly to the heart of what you want.

"First, fix in mind exactly what you're looking for. Hold this in the forefront of your mind. Flash your eyes down the page for this information only.

"Once you've found lines in the passage that 'may' yield what you're seeking, stop scanning, instantly. Shift gears into careful reading as you weigh whether you've 'really' found what you're after."

Dechant[21] writes:

"Skimming is selective reading. In skimming, the reader chooses what he wants to read. He selects those sentences, clauses, and phrases that best serve his purposes. He gets a general impression of the selection and decides on the basis of his examination whether to read the selection more intensively. He takes a quick glance at the table of contents, the index, the chapter titles, the paragraph headings, the topic sentences, and the summary. These provide valuable clues to the main idea.

"In scanning, the reader runs his eyes down the page with the purpose of finding an answer to a specific question.

"Skimming and scanning are not accelerated reading. In them the reader switches from looking to reading and so on. In fact, there may be less reading than looking, and when the person reads he reads in the usual way.

"Research tends to indicate that reading rates above eight hundred words per minute are in the nature of skimming and scanning. The reader characteristically omits part of the content and reads with considerably less comprehension."

Joseph C. Gainsburg[22] does not differentiate between skimming and scanning. He puts the term "streamlined reading" and deals with skimming and scanning only under the head 'Skimming'. The term "streamlined reading" covers only 'skimming' of various types. These types include:

(*a*) Looking up a word or words in a list.

(*b*) Locating a word or a phrase on a page of printed content.

(*c*) Locating an answer when its wording is different from the wording of the question or topic.

(*d*) Skimming to obtain the general thought.

Actually, 'scanning activity' comes under 'locational skills' which needs the fastest rates. These locational skills (scanning activity) even surpass skimming rates which are very rapid.

In skimming, the reader is not trying to find out the answer to any question. He is not trying to obtain a thorough grasp or complete mastery over any particular topic. He simply wants to know, in a very general way, what the selection is about. Here the reader makes an effort to spot certain words that can give him some hints to the meaning. His eyes deliberately skip the other words.

The Six Myths

Maxwell[23] defines skimming as the rapid processing of material to obtain key ideas, and scanning as the ability to locate specific facts and information quickly. Mention of her six myths which she suggests relate to mental attitude—an ingredient in the reading process vital to the improvement of skimming and scanning skills is very much valuable.

Myth one suggests that "I have to read every word." The second myth is that "Reading once is enough." The third, "It is sinful to skip passages in reading", the fourth being, "If I skim or read too rapidly, my comprehension will drop." Two more are like this: "Machines are necessary to improve my reading speed" and "there is something about my eyes that keeps me from reading fast."

Another popular misconception is that skimming is an activity that one lapses into when reading light material. While it is true that it is easier to read selectively on easy material, it is rare that a person actually skims or scans without a deliberate, conscious effort. In testing sessions conducted by the authors, people who felt sure that they were "skimming along at well over a thousand words per minute" were startled to find that they are well within the reading range. In discussions of skimming, other people have reported that they are sure they skim when they are reading material that they enjoy and in which they can become involved. It is seldom that a reader skims in such a situation, for as he becomes involved, he usually reverts to his characteristic or "usual" reading pattern ... Skimming and scanning are not activities to be indulged in lightly or unconsciously. On the contrary, they require conscious effort and application and are tools to be used judiciously in certain reading situations. The ability to read selectively results from the development of a number of specific skills and abilities, most of which require training and continued practice.[24]

In undertaking to acquire the super-speed of skimming the development of an entirely new attitude is a prime requisite. This new attitude is a combination of resigned willingness to pass hastily over a page without reading all that it has to say and of release from a feeling of guilt because you have not done thorough reading. For many people, considerable effort and willpower is necessary to 'break loose' and cover quantities of material without reading every word.[25]

There is much reading that must be done meticulously, of course, but most people could skim through, without loss, a great deal of the material they now read carefully. To do this, one must cut all moorings with past reading habits and recklessly take a chance at merely catching snatches of printed symbols here and there. It is necessary to cultivate an attitude of abandonment while engaging in the high-powered skill of skimming.[26]

Merits

1. If a person can skim rapidly he can improve his average reading speed and study reading speed too.
2. It is a great time and labour saver.
3. Sometimes when a student is asked to do supplementary reading for a course, the teacher will set more supplementary reading that the student can really cover at his average or study reading rate. If he skims the supplementary material (not his basic textbooks), he may be pleased and surprised to learn how much of the material he can comprehend at fast skimming rates.[27]
4. Skimming is very much useful for getting plenty of reference information.
5. Since it gives more output in very less time, readers prefer to use this skill at several occasions.
6. Professional people such as lawyers, engineers, professors, doctors, etc., need to do a large amount of reading daily. They can get rid of lots of troubles if they use this technique for keeping themselves abreast of the new development in their respective fields.
7. Even the school children, when they get sufficient training in skimming technique can use it for increasing their fund of knowledge in different content areas.
8. It also helps in book selection because the reader just skims through the pages of a book and decides whether the book is according to his taste or he can just discard it.

9. In our life, we always do not read to gain full comprehension, so if this skill gives partial comprehension and helps us in reaching the desired goal, there should not be any hesitation in using this skill freely.
10. Once a person acquires complete mastery over this skill, he is always at a very advantageous position.
11. It serves as a consolidation technique for revising reading materials just before appearing in an examination. Where your purpose is to acquire broader acquaintance with a general subject area while covering a large number of pages in a lesser time, skimming is an asset. Once mastered, it can save numerous hours of tedious, unprofitable and unnecessary reading.

Demerits

1. Skimming is such a skill which cannot be used at all times.
2. Skimming does not guarantee full comprehension.
3. It is not a full reading in the sense that the reader leaves chunks of materials in-between.
4. The reading material which has not been written in a well organised style is not suitable for skimming.
5. At some occasions, instead of doing careful reading, if a person by an oversight uses the skimming technique, he can be put to task.

If one is reading for skimming purposes, one should be satisfied even with 50 per cent comprehension. While skimming is a valuable technique for intelligent coverage of a large quantity of materials, it should not be taken as a substitute for a thorough grasp of the matter.

Skimming Is a Valuable Technique

Edward Fry[28] writes as follows:

"Business and governments often require their employees to read a large number of reports. Some of these reports are not directly related to the employee's job, and he has only a general interest in them.

Skimming will often satisfy the employee's needs and the employer's demands for this type of report reading. Adults and students often have a desire to be generally informed in such fields as political affairs or cultural developments and yet they have not the time to read much on these subjects. Skimming will often help to keep them informed in their general fields of interest without taking the time that average reading would.

"Skimming is quite useful in building up a fund of reference information. If, for example, an employee or a student is instructed to read regularly several journals or reports in a given field, the chances are that not all the articles in the journal or report will be of equal importance. It is often satisfactory if the student or employee knows merely of the existence of the article and perhaps its main idea. At a later time, in a conference or in a class, the person may cite the main idea of the article, and this will make him seem quite well informed. This is not untrue, as he is better informed than another person who has never heard of the article (perhaps because he reads so slowly that he never got round to it). If one knows of the existence of the article, one can go back and read it more carefully if the need arises."

Samuel Johnson has aptly remarked:

"Knowledge is of two kinds. We know a subject ourselves, or we know where we can find information about it."

The person who has the habit of skimming a large amount of material will invariably come across certain articles or parts of books which are of great importance to him. These parts can be read more carefully. But if he had never developed the habit of skimming, the chances are that he would never have come across the important parts of the articles.

Smith[29] rightly remarks:

"There is no greater asset to the reader of today than highly developed skill in skimming. Skimming enables a person to select quickly content which he wants to read and to discard that in which he is not interested or which is inconsequential to his purpose.

"Most adults develop some skill in skimming newspapers and magazines. This skill can be further developed to a very high degree and used profitably in doing all kinds of reading. Such development, however, requires instruction and practice if it is to function in the best capacity."

Both skimming and scanning are extremely valuable reading skills and should be developed consciously and deliberately. These two skills demand wind-like speeds. Every time a person reads not with the aim of getting cent per cent comprehension of the reading activity but he can remain satisfied even if he gets partial comprehension out of it. In certain cases partial comprehension is not bad provided it serves the purpose of the reader. Sir Francis Bacon once wrote, "Some books are to be tasted, others are to be swallowed and some few to be chewed and digested." It clearly reflects the value of applying varying reading skills to different reading materials. Some books may be just skimmed, others be read rapidly, and still others thoroughly with critical or even creative attitude.

While 'glancing' through a big bulk of reading material at fantastic speed is not a good substitute for 'learning' it, intelligent 'glancing' is much better than not glancing at all.

In skimming the intention of the reader is to get the main idea so the reader intentionally leaves out chunks of material. He willingly accepts a lowered comprehension in order to achieve a greater increase in reading speed.

A good reader believes in economy. He may not be a speed reading freak but he is an efficient reader. He has developed various reading rates for covering different reading materials. Purposes for reading differ appreciably. It is the purpose of reading which should dictate the approach. When purpose of reading can be easily achieved through skimming alone, slow and careful reading may be entirely wasteful.

The good reader takes all reading to be his province. Newspapers, periodicals, books old and new, all present themselves to him in their proper perspective; they are all grist to his mill, but they do not go into the same hopper or require the same process ... Milton may be read in words or lines, Macaulay in sentences, Thackeray in paragraphs, Conan Doyle in pages ... Skimming and rapid reading are different processes, but skimming is at times a good thing, too; even skipping, on occasion, becomes a sacred duty ... for skimming implies cream, and skipping, a foothold somewhere ... The eye of the skilled reader acts like a sixth sense, directing him to the gist of the matter in whatever form it may appear.[30]

SUMMARY

Skimming and scanning are two very important and useful advanced reading skills which help the reader to read at fantastic speeds. Skimming demands fast moving of eyes down a page in a zigzag manner, looking for some words or phrases or sentences here and there to get the kernel of the material. Scanning demands a quick answer to a specific question from the passages or chapters or even from a complete book and does not require reading of each and every word. In skimming, the intention of the reader is to get the main idea so the reader intentionally leaves out chunks of material. He willingly accepts a lowered comprehension in order to achieve a greater increase in reading. Skimming differs from scanning in that the reader is not looking for the answer to a specific question, but is only concerned with the overall picture of the reading matter. Both these skills demand wind-like speeds. Every time a person reads not with the aim of getting cent per cent comprehension of the reading activity but he can remain satisfied even if he gets partial comprehension out of it. Purposes for reading differ appreciably. It is the purpose of reading which should dictate the approach. When purpose of reading can be easily achieved through skimming alone, slow or careful reading may be entirely wasteful.

REFERENCES

1. Tinker, Miles A and McCullough, Constance M. *Teaching Elementary Reading,* Fourth Ed., Prentice-Hall, Inc., Englewood Cliffs, New Jersey, 1975, pp. 220-221.
2. ibid., pp. 220-221.
3. Schale, Florence. "Vertical Methods of Increasing Rates of Comprehension", *Journal of Reading,* 8, (April 1965), 296-300.
4. Grayum, Helen S. "An Analytic Description of Skimming: Its Purpose and Place as an Ability in Reading", in *Studies in Educations,* (Theses Abstract Series), School of Education, Indiana University, Bloomington, Indiana, 1952, pp. 137-143.

5. Moyle, Donald. *The Teaching of Reading,* 2nd ed., Ward Lock Educational, London, 1970, pp, 174-75.
6. Taylor, Stanford E. *Speed Reading ... Vs. Improved Reading Efficiency,* Educational Developmental Laboratories, New York, 1962, pp. 34-37.
7. Taylor, Stanford E and Frackenpohl, Helen. *EDL Skimmer,* Educational Developmental Laboratories, New York, 1961, pp. 9-16.
8. ibid., pp. 9-16.
9. Smith, Nila Banton. "Speed Reading: Benefits and Dangers", in John Downing (ed.). *The First International Reading Symposium Oxford 1964,* Cassel and Company, Ltd., London, 1966, pp. 209-234.
10. ibid., pp. 209-234.
11. Tinker, Miles A. "Recent Studies of Eye Movements in Reading", *Psychol Bull.,* 55, (1958), 215-231.
12. Grayum, Helen S. "Skimming in Reading: A Fine Art for Modern Needs", *Nat' I Assoc. See. Sch. Prin. Bill.,* 39 (212), (1955), 26-34.
13. Spache, George D and Berg, Paul C. *Faster Reading for Business,* T.Y. Crowell, New York, 1958.
14. Gainsburg, Joseph C. *Advanced Skills in Reading,* Book 1, The Macmillan Company, New York, 1962, pp. 165 and 170.
15. Smith, Nila Banton. *Reading Instruction for Today's Children,* Prentice-Hall, Inc., Englewood Cliffs, New Jersey, 1963, pp. 378-379.
16. Spache, George D and Berg, Paul C. *The Art of Efficient Reading,* The Macmillan Company, New York, 1966, pp. 53-54.
17. Thomas, Ellen Lamar and Robinson, H. Alan. *Improving Reading, in Every Class,* Abridged Ed., Allyn and Bacon; Inc., Boston, 1972, (Fourth Printing, July 1974), pp. 148-49 and 192.
18. Spache, George D and Spache, Evelyn B. *Reading in the Elementary Schools,* Allyn and Bacon, Inc., Boston, 1969, p. 281.
19. Thomas, Ellen Lamar and Robinson, H. Alan. *Improving Reading in Every Class,* ... op. cit.
20. ibid.
21. Dechant, Emerald. *Reading Improvement in the Secondary School,* Prentice-Hall, Inc., Englewood Cliffs, New Jersey, 1973, pp. 326-327.
22. Gainsburg, Joseph C. *Advanced Skills in Reading,* Book 1, The Macmillan Company, New York, 1962, pp. 165-170.
23. Maxwell, Martha in Peter A. Sherer: "Skimming and Scanning: De-Mything the Process with a College Student", *Journal of Reading* 19 (1), (October 1975), pp. 24-27.
24. Taylor, Stanford E; Frackenpohl, Helen and Berg, Paul C. *Skimming and Scaning,* Teacher's Guide, Educational Developmental Laboratories, A Division of the McGraw-Hill Book Company, New York, 1968, pp. 12-13.
25. Smith, Nila Banton. "Speed Readings; Benefits and Dangers"... op. cit.
26. ibid.
27. Fry, Edward. *Teaching Faster Reading—A Manual,* The University Press, Cambric 1963, 59-61.

28. ibid.

29. Smith, Nila Banton. *Reading Instruction for Today's Children,* Prentice-Hall, Inc., Englewood Cliffs, New Jersey, 1963, pp. 378-379.

30. Anonymous Writer, Atlantic Monthly, July 1902, quoted by Walter James Moore in *A Laboratory Study of the Relation of Selected Elements to the Skimming Process in Silent Reading,* Doctoral Dissertation, Syracuse University, 1955.

6

STUDY TECHNIQUES

Reading is like eating peanuts: once you begin, you tend to go on and on. Every book stands by itself, like a one-family house, but books are like houses in a city. Although they are separate, together they all add up to something; they are connected with each other and with other cities. The same ideas, or related ones, turn up in different places; the human problems that repeat themselves in life repeat themselves in literature, but with different solutions according to different authors who wrote at different times. Books influence each other; they link the past and the present and the future and have their own generations, like families. Wherever you start reading you connect yourself with one of the families of ideas, and, in the long run, you not only find out about the world and the people in it, you find out about yourself, too.[1]

There are several ways of reading—namely, as many ways as there are things to read. To study effectively, you must be able to develop different types of reading skills in different ways at different times.

Study Reading—Is There Such a Thing?

Study reading is active reading. An active reader is always thinking not only about what the words say but what the words mean.

If in his study the reader is concerned only with what the author says, he will soon find himself at the mercy of the printed page. His thinking must be extended to reacting to, challenging and interpreting what is read. Students must be shown there is more to study than merely reading the pages of an assignment. Challenging an author will involve looking for appropriateness of assumptions, adequateness of supporting evidence and relevance of particular information for the reader's purpose. The thoughtful reader must recognise that as hc brings himself into what he reads it is important for him to understand his own biases.[2]

In order that students acquire information through their own efforts, they must learn to provide self-direction. They must learn efficient ways of pursuing their objectives once they have established them. They must learn to be selective as they receive large quantities of information while separating ideas and retaining those which they need to complete their tasks. Pupils must learn to make decisions, test alternatives, reconstruct ideas. In addition to using the skills of word recognition, literal and inferential comprehension, and critical evaluation—skills that apply to all kinds of reading—pupils who engage in study activities must become efficient users of sets of skills that have special relevance for them. These sets are called study or reading-study skills.[3]

Complete reading is said to involve four steps: recognition, understanding, reaction and integration. Ideally, the reading a student does will influence and direct some future activity. In a very real sense, than, whenever the student integrates what he is reading, he is studying. This may be the ultimate aim in comprehension. Gray[4] points out that integration is "the heart of the learning act in reading".

Integrative reading is commonly identified with study-type reading. Herber[5] defines study skills as work skills that produce useful knowledge for a learner; they are reading skills especially adapted to execute particular tasks. They help us to develop ideas.

Russell[6] defines study skills as including skill in locating, selecting, using and evaluating information, ability to adjust method and rate of reading to the purpose of reading and to the nature of the material and the skill in retaining what is read.

A very rich knowledge of vocabulary, intellectual level, past experiences of the reader help a long way in getting the meaning of the printed page. The person who is equally good at all kinds of reading is an exception rather than the rule. Different kinds of reading require different kinds of mindsets and reading habits.

Various Study Techniques

Dividends can be tremendous if streamlined habits of reading are developed through better study techniques. Study techniques help people to become systematic readers. These techniques have changed overly conscientious readers who tried to retain everything on the page into "differentiating" readers, better able to select out what is important to remember. They have even transformed students who used to dream their way through the chapter into alert, participating readers.

A number of study techniques have been evolved by different authorities in the field. Some of the widely used techniques are:

(*a*) OK4R (Overview, Key ideas, Read, Recall, Reflect, Review)

(*b*) PQRST (Preview, Question, Read, Summarise, Test)

(*c*) SQ3R (Survey, Question, Read, Recite, Review)

(*d*) PQ4R (Preview, Question, Read, Reflect, Recite, Review)

A detailed description of all these techniques has been given on the following pages.

(*a*) OK4R

Walter Pauk[7] developed a reading technique for prose, poetry and drama called EVOKER system—explore, vocabulary, oral reading, key ideas, evaluation and recapitulation. Later he developed the OK4R[8] method—Overview, Key ideas, Read, Recall, Reflect and Review. He gives the following outline of the OK4R study technique.

	O	Overview. Take about five minutes to read introductory and summary paragraphs of the assignment. Then read centre and side headings, or topic sentences if there are no headings, to determine general content
BEFORE		and sequence of topics. Locate the main divisions.

K Key ideas. Distinguish key ideas from secondary ideas and supporting materials. Convert headings or topic sentences into questions—a sure way to become involved in the author's ideas.

DURING R^1 Read. Read the section or paragraphs consecutively to answer your questions and to see how supporting materials clarify or prove key points. Pay close attention to transitional words and phrases. If you are reading persuasive materials, keep asking yourself: What is the evidence? Does it prove the point? Is there enough support? Do I believe this? Why or why not? If you are reading exposition, ask yourself the following questions: What is the main point in this section? Does this example make the main point clear? Can I think of other examples?

AFTER

R^2 Recall. After reading, test your memory and understanding. Without looking at the book, try to say or write the main points and supporting materials in your own words. If you cannot do so immediately after reading, you cannot hope to tomorrow in class or next week in an exam. Now—but not before—take brief summary notes in your notebook or underline key points in your book and make "recall" notes in the margins. Remember to understand first, then write.

R^3 Reflect. Recall will help fix the material in your mind. To make it really yours, go further: Think about it. Relating new facts and ideas to others you already know gives added meaning to new and old knowledge and establishes both more firmly in your mind. This is the essence of all creative thinking: the discovery of new relationships and new significance.

R^4 Review. To keep material fresh in mind, review it periodically. Re-read your notes and say over the sequence of main ideas and supporting materials until you have them once more firmly in mind. Mastery is a never-ending process.

(*b*) PQRST

Spache and Berg[9] introduced PQRST method which involves Preview, Question, Read, Summarise and Test as the five sequenced steps. The details of the steps are as follows:

P: Preview the selection. Read the title, headings, first and last sentences of paragraphs. Introductory or summary paragraphs should be read. Previewing is a thinking process preceding reading. It may give all of the information needed or it may indicate just what part of the selection is needed.

Q: Raise question about the content during the previewing. Jot down some questions from the preview. Headings can be made into questions.

R: Read to answer the questions posed in steps P and Q.

S: Summarise by making brief notes based on answers to preview questions. Find the main idea for each paragraph. Select a final main idea for the entire selection. A written summary is not always necessary.

T: Test understanding by attempting to answer preview questions without looking at the notes or the selection. Try to phrase some questions that an instructor might ask.

(*c*) SQ3R

The SQ3R study technique has been originated by Francis P. Robinson who has been doing research in the field of reading study skills for over 30 years. The SQ3R method of reading presents an excellent example of a systematic approach to reading that is based upon experimental findings in psychological studies of learning, perception, retention, motivation, etc. The steps involved in SQ3R are Survey, Question, Read, Recite and Review.

S: Surveying is the first step in the SQ3R method and is the process of getting acquainted with the broad outlines, the chapter title, the main headings, the topic sentences, and the summary.

A good student gets an overall picture of what he is reading or studying. The reason is obvious. The driver consults a road map before venturing on a trip. The race driver drives the course many times before the actual race. The diner surveys a menu and in rapid fashion he notices the food items, appetisers and drinks, and the prices do not escape him. The baseball player checks the infield for chuckholes, and the General surveys the terrain before initiating his attack. Each of these persons want to know what lies ahead so they may proceed with the proper technique. The student must know what type of article he is reading before he can choose his techniques well.[10]

Kravitz[11] suggests that you should look for all of the following items before you begin to read.

(*i*) *Boldface Type:* This is the heavy, dark, large print at the beginning of each chapter, section and paragraph. Look at the name of the chapter and the section heading.

(*ii*) *Pictures with captions:* The picture and its caption which is the explanation of the picture will help in knowing about the material you will soon read.

(*iii*) *Charts:* A chart will give you much information at a glance. When you read the chart before you read the text, you will have much information to help you understand the paragraphs.

(*iv*) *Drawings with captions:* A drawing is considered the same as a picture when you survey the material before you understand the chapter or section.

(*v*) *Maps and diagrams:* A map or diagram will explain many paragraphs of written material if you look at it before you begin to read. A map or diagram may reduce half a page of writing into one small drawing.

(*vi*) *Summary:* At the end of most chapters there is a summary. The summary tells very briefly the information that is in the chapter. After you have read the summary, you will usually have a very good idea of the main topics in the chapter.

(*vii*) *Questions:* The author adds questions to his chapter to direct your attention to some of the important ideas. Be sure to look at the questions before you read the selection. This step will help you to be ready for the new thoughts you are about to read.

Spache and Berg[12] refer to this phase as "previewing". The reader tries to see the general outline of the study task. In doing this he may read the topic sentences and the headings. The student should not rush through this first step but should preview rather thoughtfully, trying to relate each heading to its main ideas and to relate each section to the rest of the chapter. In this phase of good study the student "warms-up" to the task ahead.

One of the major premises of many present-day theories of learning is that meaningful material is easier to learn and remember than is non-meaningful material. This principle is highly pertinent to learning through reading. One important way in which a reader can increase the meaningfulness of any material for himself is by previewing the material to be read before reading it in detail. This process will enable him to have some prior understanding of the content and of the major trends in discussion. He will be less apt to let appearance of the trees dull his perception of the forest.[13]

Our children are not used to previewing before reading. Most of them have not even heard of this skill. Danskin and Burnett[14] remark, "Many high school and college students, among the brightest have not learned to preview an article, chapter or book before reading it in detail."

McClusky divided 118 college students into two equated groups; one group was shown how to skim over headings and summaries and the other was not shown. When these two groups were given a selection to read, the trained group read 24 per cent faster than, and just as accurately as, the control group.[15]

Q: The second step in the SQ3R technique is 'Question'. Here the reader has to turn the main headings or even subheadings of the chapter into questions. Keeping these questions in view the reader has to approach the selection or the chapter while reading. This is a very important step. This becomes a very difficult step when the reader does not find subheadings in many of the selections which he has to read for study purposes. Still all the main paragraphs contain some material in an organised form so as to be able to answer some questions which have been directly prepared, keeping in view the material contained in these paragraphs. This questioning step keeps the motivational level of the reader to the highest ebb. Since in this step the reader himself is the lord who forms questions for himself, there is more satisfaction to him and also it is without any external imposition.

The value of asking and attempting to answer questions has been established by research. Holmes, equating two groups of college students, presented one group with questions based on the material to be read. Both groups read the same English literature and science materials. Not only did the group with the list of questions learn better, but a re-test two weeks later indicated that they retained better.[16] As early as 1922, Judd and Buswell[17] referred to the value of questions. They suggested that waiting for the teacher to raise questions at examination time frequently does not lead to any well-ordered plan of attack on the content of the passage read. Students should be encouraged to ask themselves intelligent questions and be shown how to find appropriate answers for them.

Melnik[18] notes that questions establish a basis for identifying and clarifying the purpose for reading. Taba and others suggest that the teacher's questions circumscribe the mental operations that students can perform and determine what points they can explore and what modes of thought they can learn.[19] Frederick[20] however, found that the introduction of vocabulary terms and questions prior to reading did not result in better learning or retention on the part of students.

Rothkopf [21] suggests that the set of questions that the students expect largely determine learning rather than immediate feedback of knowledge of results and that questions asked after the reading are more important for understanding and retention than those asked before.

Holmes set up two large equated groups of college students and had them read selections about science and history. One group was given twenty questions "before" reading. As might be expected, the group given the questions did better in answering them, but they also did as well or better on additional questions. The advantage was particularly great on tests given two weeks after reading. Still another study by Washburne indicates the best placement for such questions. In this study 1456 high school students were divided into several groups of equal ability. Questions were given to the different groups as follows: at the beginning of reading, at the end of reading, each question just before the material answering it, and no questions. The test contained questions already provided as well as other questions. Of these different placements—two proved most effective; all questions at the beginning of the reading and each question just before it was answered in the material.[22]

It goes beyond doubt that questions provide a certain readiness for reading. They work as a motivational force for reading.

Melnik lists two main functions of questions. As a diagnostic tool, the unstructured question permits the teacher to observe the variety of individual responses: how the student approaches the reading passage; his tendency to relate ideas or perhaps to focus on isolated details; his ability to organise; his tendency to let emotions and prejudices influence his comprehension. As an instructional tool, the question helps the student to identify the author's pattern of thought or to clarify meaning. Questions are most effective in enhancing delayed and immediate recall for the largest number of meaning values. The question technique tends to surpass both careful reading without questions and re-reading of the same material.[23]

R: Purposeful reading is involved in the third step 'Read'. What is the reader expected to do in this step? Apart from careful reading he should keep the following points in mind.[24]

1. Have a definite reason for his reading.
2. Define clearly the problem that he wishes to solve.
3. Focus his attention on the main points.
4. Try to group the supporting details with the main idea.
5. Keep in mind the nature of the assignment.
6. Pay special attention to illustrations of all kinds, graphs, maps, charts, etc.
7. Be a flexible reader, adjusting his rate to the purpose of the reading and nature of the material.

8. Try to remember that he is seeking to answer questions.

This step occurs after he has read all the pages twice, once to survey and another time to make questions. This is the style which differentiates between simple study reading in which the reader reads the chapter slowly one or more times reading straight.

R: The fourth step in this process is 'Recite' which is literally a self-examination. Here the reader recites the answers to the questions which he had posed to himself in the second step without referring to his notes. It is only when he fails to answer the questions that he should refer back to his notes or books.

Bacon said, "If you read anything over twenty times you will not learn it by heart so easily as if you were to read it only ten, trying to repeat it between whiles, and when memory failed looking at the book." Recitation does not mean word for word repetition, or learning by heart but it is only outlining the substance of a passage. The outline provides the framework into which more details can be fitted in subsequent recitation. Recitation aids concentration.

Unquestionably, inability to concentrate one's attention on the meaning of what one is reading is a very important reason for poor concentration. But lack of ability to concentrate is itself a result of causes, a name for the fact that the individual is unable to adjust to the requirements of the reading situation. Inability to concentrate is not in itself an explanation. Before one can take practical measures, one should try to find out what the reasons are that make it difficult for the person to concentrate.[25]

Self-recitation makes a number of contributions to effective learning. The student is immediately aware of how well he reads, how accurately he accomplished his purpose, and whether he can express his new found knowledge in his own words. If he can verbalise his knowledge to his satisfaction, he can generally explain or recite to another. Recitation is the heart of effective study; it is the seeking of answers to self-imposed questions and of putting new learnings into one's own words.[26]

When we recite we recall, and recall is a powerful aid to retention. Recitation also directs our attention to specific questions, thereby aiding concentration. Concentration is a by-product of having a goal that challenges the mind.[27]

Generally it is recommended that the recitation should occur as soon as possible after the reading. Weigand and Blake[28] emphasise two other aspects of effective recitation and study: (*a*) whenever possible, substitute understanding for rote memorisation and recite in your own words, and (*b*) if you "must" memorise (formulas, poetry, etc.), overlearn at once, that is, repeat the piece of material several times after you have proved to yourself that you know it.

Since recall has obvious significance for learning, let's examine some of the specific benefits that may accrue from it. The following five points are suggested.[29]

1. ... the conscious use of recall during the process of study demands that the acts of reading be effortful ... It obliges him (the student) to set specific goals and to make an immediate evaluation of his progress towards them (studies show that this immediate evaluation of knowledge of one's success is a positive incentive to learning).
2. ... recall, that is followed by a re-reading, gives the learner a chance to check immediately on the accuracy of his learning. Correct information is confirmed and incorrect information is rejected.
3. ... when the learner recalls material by himself he builds up confidence in his ability to recall it at a later time. There is less chance that panic will rob him of his learning when he tries to draw on it for an examination or a real-life situation.
4. Recall lets the learner assess what he has learned, and thus prevents useless practice on what he already knows.
5. Recall helps the learner to organise his knowledge into meaningful relationships.

R: Review is the final step in this technique which provides scope for spaced practice and thereby aiding retention. Dechant[30] suggests two methods of review; symbolical review and review by re-impression. Re-impression is the type of review that occurs when the person re-reads. Symbolical review is done through recall, self-recitation, class discussion, tests, summaries and lecture notes. This type of review encourages thinking, assimilation, integration and organisation. It is a review with a purpose and with an eye on application.

Studies show that with a single reading the typical reader gets only about 60 per cent of the ideas asked on an immediate quiz, and with immediate re-readings is able to raise his comprehension score only to about 65 per cent. Another study of several thousand high school students showed that there is rapid forgetting after reading: within two weeks after an initial reading only 20 per cent is remembered of what was known immediately after reading. This study also showed that a testing-type review immediately after reading was very helpful in reducing forgetting, e.g., instead of 80 per cent there was only a 20 per cent loss.[31]

Several review times, rather than one lengthy session, should be scheduled. A review time should be scheduled separately from study time. A definite segment of the lesson should be assigned to each review time so that the task looks possible of completion, and does not lead to procrastination.[32]

Stroud[33] has pointed out that review should be more than a review or re-reading of materials. It should result in an extension and organisation of what has been learned. Review should be a critical re-examination with a goal of integrating the content and acquiring useful generalisations. Review may serve to relate material studied at one time to material studied at another with the result that both sets of material are better understood and better remembered.

The distribution of study sessions will vary according to the functions the study is to serve: (1) obtaining clear comprehension or quick learning, or (2) renewing learning through review. Suffice to say here that the rate of forgetting and the value of review near examination time are prime factors in determining the distribution of review sessions. When it comes to trying for the first time to understand some different problem or to learn some task requiring exact reproduction as in a poem or foreign vocabulary, an entirely different distribution of learning session is needed. In the latter case, enough time should be taken on the first reading to acquire a meaningful view of the total task. Evidence already discussed indicates that, rather than re-reading the lesson, an immediate effort at self-recitation is more effective. How long should the student then wait for the next session? If he waits too long there will be so much forgetting that studying again will seem like a new task. If the next session is too soon, the factors of fatigue and boredom may be operative. One experiment sheds some light on this problem. Different equated groups tried reading a lesson four times, with the reading sessions distributed as follows: four times in one session, once a session each three hours apart, once a session each one day apart, and once a session each three days apart. The four study sessions three hour apart proved to be the best of the four plans.[34]

Fry[35] states: Overall, the SQ3R method has a good deal of practice and repetition built into it. The student first sees the material when he surveys; he sees it once more when he formulates his questions; he sees it for a third time when he reads more deliberately; and a fourth time when he answers his questions. Finally, a fifth reinforcement occurs in the review. The review stage, coming as it does at a later time, involves the principle of "spaced practice."

A summary of the steps involved in SQ3R method is given below:[36]

Q: What does SQ3R mean?

A: Survey, Question, Read, Recite and Review.

Q: What does 'Survey' mean?

A: Turn all the pages in the chapter being studied, see how long it is, and get a general idea of the content.

Q: What is meant by 'Question'?

A: Write down questions on each main point in the chapter. Base the questions on the main points, which can be deduced from the sub-headings or extracted by skimming.

Q: What does 'Read' mean?

A: Read the chapter completely to answer the questions. Note that reading is not done first.

Q: What is meant by 'Recite'?

A: Answer the questions completely, either orally to another person or in writing, putting answers in your own words.

Q: What does 'Review' mean?

A: Some days later the material should be revised, possibly by quickly re-reading the chapter, and/or trying to answer the questions, looking up all wrong or partial answers.

Donald[37] found that the use of the SQ3R method (a method of integrative reading) develops better power of organisation, association and critical thinking.

(*d*) PQ4R

Another technique PQ4R for study reading has been propounded by Thomas and Robinson.[38] PQ4R is a package of techniques that should be effective in improving the reading of chapter-length materials when the student's purpose is a thorough understanding of the content. It should help him comprehend better, concentrate better, and retain better. The steps in the procedure are: Preview, Question, Read, Reflect, Recite and Review. In presenting this technique, the writers have leaned heavily on Robinson's classic book, *Effective Study.*

PQ4R is applicable to the reading of informational chapters in science, health, history, civics, contemporary problems, geography, sociology, economics, philosophy, journalism, homemaking, vocational education and industrial arts, business law, accounting, music appreciation, music history, music harmony, art appreciation, art history, and other courses—and in English when the chapters are expository. It is adaptable to expository passages in mathematics, to informational passages in a second language, and to articles in periodicals.[39]

Study techniques go with the assumption that the reader has developed the skills of phrase reading, understands the structure of a paragraph and can identify key words. These methods are efficient in developing comprehension for study purposes, provided the reader is guided step by step through the method beginning with easy materials or with the subject matter with which he has little or no conceptual or vocabulary difficulty. It is suggested that to begin with, the reader should use the study technique with one content field so that he may master the procedure and coordinate the many skills required. Gradually he may be advised to switch over to a second content field with slightly difficult material. The reader is free to try any technique or a mixture of the two techniques with slight modification as per his interest, purpose or material at hand.

Allied Study Skills

Study reading requires maximum comprehension. Here the reader wants maximum retention too. In fact, he desires to remember all, or at least a big percentage of what he has read for a long period of time. Study reading is a slow and careful reading where the reader needs time to think about what he is reading. The reader wants to reflect, he also wants to relate it to other previously known materials. Quite often the reader wants to engage in some additional but very useful study skills. These are note making, summarising and outlining, and underlining. All these devices for perfect study are very much useful and when done conscientiously and not mechanically, they aid in reading comprehension and retention.

Note making: Note making is a skill which demands your full, active participation. Note making is different from note taking. To take notes suggests a passive procedure of recording words 'verbatim' which is like a secretary taking dictation. To make notes demands your complete attention. While making notes, one must be alert to the pattern of thought, its direction and development and also must discriminate between what is important and what is not. No doubt this type of serious involvement on the part of the reader makes note making a difficult process but this is the activity which makes note making a worthwhile achievement. Notes help us recall and also summarise information. These help us understand the material in the total context rather as a separate series of passages or chapters.

A recent survey of college students shows that three-fourth of those who fail major subjects in college lack this skill. Some time ago, an investigation at the Carnegie Institute of Technology showed that

80 per cent of the Institute's freshmen had no preparation in note taking. Taking notes as a basis for memoranda, letters, and reports is common practice in business and industry.[40]

A study made during World War II of superior college students referred for specialised training showed that these students had been making their A's and B's more by strength of intellect than by efficient study skills. When these students were asked to read and take notes their "work rate" was only ninety-three words per minute, and the quality of their notes was little better than average ... Other studies show that readers often do not clearly comprehend ideas as they read along, and the rapid succession of ideas in reading tends to interfere with what is comprehended because of retroactive inhibition. So there is need for a system to check on comprehension while reading and also to help in fixing ideas better in memory. Note-taking can be used for this purpose, but the manner in which most students take notes is of little help. That is, studies shows that students tend to copy down phrases as soon as they find an important idea, and if the phrase is in italics they may write it down without understanding the point. Many students do not like to take notes because they write in complete sentences, which markedly slows down their reading speed.[41]

Effective note making is a high level study skill. This requires a combination of digestion, learning and putting into practice one's organising abilities.

Dechant[42] remarks:

"It is not uncommon to find a conscientious student failing to get significant results from note making. Perhaps the notes themselves are adequate, but the student has not taken the pains to organise them. He has written them on any piece of paper available. Unfortunately, when the time comes for review, he can no longer locate the odd bits of paper or, if he can find them, he no longer knows what comes first and what comes next.

"Some students may be too wordy. Simplicity is the key to good note making. Thoroughness, however, should not be ignored. The student must learn to take enough notes so that if after the lecture he spends a few moments on them, he can organise them into a representation of the lecture or of his reading. This is impossible when he takes notes only over those elements that he does not understand."

Eisner and Rohde[43] found that making notes after the lecture was just as effective as making them during the lecture. Perhaps if students were trained to delay note making, retention would generally improve. Notes are only an aid to learning, not learning itself.

There are three basic forms of note making.[44]

1. The paragraph—This is probably most easily developed, but it frequently is not the best organised. Each paragraph represents a new idea.
2. The sentence—This is better than the paragraph form, in that it attempts to organise the material by stating a series of sentences. It thus may also be easier to use in review.
3. The outline—This provides the best opportunity for organisation.

Kollaritsch[45] suggests an outline method of note making that involves relatively little writing. Instead of detailed description, the method consists of (*a*) stating the section heading of a chapter, noting the page on which it is found; (*b*) noting what each paragraph in the chapter is about, and what kinds of things the student needs to remember from the paragraph without writing out the details, (e.g., definition of parapsychology) and (*c*) reviewing immediately after reading, and indicating by a check if he can recall what each written heading elicits without referring to the text. The same procedure is used for review.

In addition to its value for review, note taking performs a useful function in enforcing selective, thoughtful reading. In taking good notes one must try to select the major from the minor points, decide what is worth recording, consider the relation of one idea to another, and rephrase the author's idea into a condensed but accurate restatement in one's own words.[46]

Summarising and Outlining: Summarising is an art, a skill which an efficient reader must learn. Summaries help to preserve the main points and essential facts in a brief, consolidated form. Summaries should always be easy to handle with. These should not contain some lines from here and some from there not reflecting the general theme of the passage or chapter. Outlining is also a way of organising information. It is very closely related to summarising.

No skill is more essential to the student of today than the ability to write an effective summary of what he reads. When all of one's study is from a single textbook, written notes are not absolutely essential. But when one's study involves consulting a variety of sources, most of which are in a library and cannot easily be taken out again when one wants to review, a satisfactory summary is indispensable.[47]

Dechant[48] remarks:

"Outlining is not easy. Many speakers and writers do not have a clear-cut outline. Others, because not all students immediately grasp what is said, repeat or elaborate at great length. This may tend to make their presentation, seem unorganised. As the student attempts to outline such a presentation, he needs to ignore the unimportant details. He must select the essentials from the non-essentials.

"Once the student understands the organisation, he is ready to put this organisation into an outline form. He starts by listing the major points. Points of lesser importance that support the main ideas are indented. Indentation gives clues to the organisation."

Underlining: Underlining is a very useful skill. It is only possible if the reader's own book is being used. One should not make use of this skill on library books or borrowed books. When underlining, the reader should have a code of symbols that he can use consistently. The topic sentence may have two lines under it, the supporting details may have only one line under the key words. Many a time, students make use of a vertical bar in the margin to indicate an area of importance. An S in the margin may indicate that at that point the writer has summarised what is being said. Similarly, a question mark in the margin indicates that there is a section that the reader does not understand. A circle is used to indicate new and technical words in the paragraph.

Dechant[49] writes:

"Many students use underlining key words and phrase in a book to organise what they have read. Unfortunately, the technique used is frequently not good. The student reads and underlines words and phrases in a hit-and-miss fashion. He finds out too late that his underlining was not planned. In short, it does not show the organisation of what was read. When the student returns to the underlining later, he finds that he can no longer decipher the reasons for underlining. Underlining thus may become a poor substitute for the thinking and organising that accompanies good reading."

Proper understanding requires the student:

1. To survey the chapter.
2. To read the chapter.
3. To mentally familiarise himself with the organisation of the chapter.
4. To underline main ideas and supporting details after having read each paragraph.
5. To underline only those words and phrases that actually indicates the organisation of the paragraph.

Why is marking a book indispensable to reading it? First, it keeps you awake. (And I don't mean merely conscious; I mean wide awake). In the second place, reading, if it is active, is thinking, and thinking tends to express itself in words, spoken or written. The marked book is usually the thought-through book. Finally, writing helps you remember the thoughts the author expressed.[50]

Remembering What Is Read

Study-type reading is often called intensive reading. It is very careful, rather slow reading with considerable emphasis upon remembering details. This is the kind of reading that is necessary when studying for immediate detailed tests or recitations.[51]

Nevertheless, not all reading in a textbook needs to be, nor even should be, intensive reading. Gates[52] calls for greater stress on a flexible approach to reading. Reading should vary in speed from very slow to moderate to very fast—from detailed study to skimming and scanning. The student should be able to shift from reading to recall and *vice versa.* If he has learned to adapt his reading to the nature of the specific problem being met, his purposes and the nature of the paragraph or chapter will determine the type of reading that he will use. Even in comprehension there must be flexibility. Certain parts of chapters of a textbook, perhaps most of it, must be read intensively, but frequently much can profitably be skimmed. The flexible reader reads rapidly or even skips those parts that are trivial, familiar or unrelated to his goals and purposes.

Unfortunately the slow learner generally retains less than the rapid learner. McGeoch and Irion[53] conclude that, generally, individual differences in learning are reflected in individual differences in retention. Possibly this is because the rapid learner is better able to see the relationships and principles that are involved in whatever he learns. Long ago Pyle[54] reported that the fast learner remembers words, objects, pictures, syllables, and connected thought-passages better than the slow learner and is more accurate. However, individual differences usually are not great when time required for re-learning is compared with time required for initial learning. Thus experiments have indicated that individuals tend to differ less in retention than in the ability to learn. However, even this minor point in favour of the slow learner may be due to the fact that in requiring much longer to learn, he overlearns certain portions of the task before he learns the entire task. Certainly the slow learner gains no general advantage in retention from his slowness.

There are marked individual differences in ability to recall the essentials of what has been read even among readers who all understand fairly well what they are reading while they read it. It is a common complaint at all academic levels that the student cannot remember what he has read. Some people do remember better than others. In fact all individuals can learn to remember better if they are trained to employ certain accepted principles of learning. Tinker and McCullough[55] suggest the following set of principles:

1. It is easier for you to remember material that you read with a high degree of understanding. When material is only partially comprehended, it is difficult or impossible to recall it.
2. Read with a positive attitude, with intention to remember. Reading in a lackadaisical manner fosters inattention and

daydreaming. It often helps in concentration to read at a rate slightly faster than you find comfortable.

3. Try to think while you read. Note ideas relevant to the reading purpose and their relationships. Material organised by the reader as he goes along promotes easier recall. Piekarz[56] noted that the more able readers, grasped implied as well as literal meanings. The poorer readers had difficulty distinguishing between what the author said and what he thought. Again, this implies ability on the part of the reader to understand what he is reading.
4. Select items relevant to the reasons for which you are reading. Concentrate on these. Not all the facts can be remembered. The efficient reader is one who tries to retain only essential points.
5. Outline in note form as you read, or underline topic sentences and relevant supporting facts, or make marginal notes of points considered important. Shortly after reading, go over the notes again, underline parts, and note continuities and relationships.
6. Re-read your notes at least once, and afterwards review them periodically to ensure retention.
7. After reading a body of material—not too much at once—pause and try to recall the essential points in it. Recite them to yourself and at the same time note how the ideas tie in with one another.

In general, if one is to remember what he has read, he should (*a*) read actively with a definite purpose, (*b*) attend to relevant items and their implications, (*c*) outline what he reads, (*d*) review his notes periodically, and (*e*) recite to himself the important points.[57]

SUMMARY

Study reading is active reading. An active reader is always thinking not only about what the words say but what the words mean. Dividends can be tremendous if streamlined habits of reading are developed through better study techniques. Study techniques help people to become systematic readers. OK4R, PQRST, SQ3R and PQ4R are some of the very useful study techniques which go a long way in improving study reading habits among the readers. These techniques have changed overly conscientious readers who tried to retain everything on the page in "differentiating" readers, better able to select out what is important to remember. They have even transformed students who used to dream their way through the chapter into alert participating readers. Study techniques go with the assumption that the reader has developed the skills of phrase reading, understands the structure of a paragraph and can identify key words. These methods are efficient in developing comprehension for study purposes, provided the reader is guided step by step through the method beginning with easy materials or with the subject matter with which he has little or no vocabulary difficulty. Study reading requires maximum comprehension where the reader wants maximum retention too. Here the reader wants to go with a slow speed. He wants to think about what he is reading. He also wants to reflect and relate his reading to previously known material. For this, quite often the reader wants to engage in some additional but very much useful study skills. These are note making, summarising and outlining, and underlining. For a thorough grasp of the subject matter, study techniques with a combination of study skills can profitably be employed.

REFERENCES

1. Cerf, Bennet. "The Pleasures of Reading", in Alfred, Stefferud, (ed.), *The Wonderful World of Books,* New World Library of World Literature, Inc., New York, 1952, p. 25.
2. Fay, Leo. "How Can We Develop Reading Study Skills for the Different Curriculum Areas?" *The Reding Teacher,* 6 (6), (March 1953), 12-18.
3. Karlin, Robert. *Teaching Elementary Reading—Principles and Strategies,* Harcourt Brace Jovanovich, Inc., New York, 1971, p. 233.
4. Gray, W. S. "Is your Reading Programme a Good One", *University of Cansas Conference of Reading,* International Reading Association, 12, October 1957.
5. Herber, Harold L. "Study Skills: Reading to Develop, Remember and Use Ideas", *Reading in the Content Areas,* Syracuse University, Syracuse, New York, 1969, pp. 13-21.
6. Russell, David H. *Children Learn to Read,* Ginn and Company, New York, 1961, p. 359.
7. Pauk, Walter. "On Scholarship: Advice to School Students", *The Reading Teacher,* 7, (November 1963), 73-78.
8. Pauk, Walter, "Techniques for Textbook Study", *Reading Improvement,* 6 (Spring 1969), 1-7.
9. Spache, George D and Berg, Paul C. *The Art of Efficient Reading* 2nd ed., The Macmillan Company, New York, p. 93.
10. Dechant, Emerald. *Reading Improving in the Secondary School,* Prentice-Hall, Inc., Englewood Cliffs, New Jersey, 1973, pp. 263-267, 274 and 276-277.

11. Kravitz, Alvin. "Teaching the Essential Reading Skills in Social Studies" in Figurel, J. Allen (ed.), *Forging Ahead in Reading,* International Reading Association, Newark, Delaware, 1967, pp. 223-228.

12. Spache, George D and Berg, Paul C. *The Art of Efficient Reading,* Macmillan Company, New York, 1955, pp. 29-30.

13. Dechant, Emerald (ed.). *De-tec-tion and Cor-rec-tion of Read-ing Dif-fi-cul-ties,* Appleton-Century Crofts, New York, 1971, p. 378.

14. Danskin, D. G and Burnett, C. W in Dechant, Emerald (ed.), *Detec-tion and Cor-rec-tion of Read-ing Dif-fi-cul-ties,* Appleton-Century Crofts, New York, 1971, p. 370.

15. Robinson, F. P. "Study Skills for Superior Students in Secondary School", in Adams, W. Royce., *Increasing Reading Speed,* The Macmillan Company, New York, 1969, pp. 193-196.

16. Holmes, Eleanor. "Reading Guided by Questions Versus Careful Reading and Re-reading Without Questions", *School Review,* 39, (May 1931), 361-371.

17. Judd, Charles H and Buswell, G. T. *Silent Reading: A Study of Various Types,* Supplementary Educational Monographs, No. 23, University of Chicago Press, Chicago, 1922, p. 44.

18. Melnik, Amelia. "The Formulation of Questions as an Instructional Diagnostic Tool", *Reading in Inquiry,* International Reading Association, 10, (1965).

19. Taba, Hilda; *et. al. Thinking in Elementary School Children,* Cooperative Research Project, No. 1574, San Francisco State College, San Francisco, 1964, p. 53.

20. Frederick, E. C. "A Study of the Effects of Certain Readiness Activities of Concept Learning", *Unpublished doctoral dissertation,* Syracuse University, 1968.

21. Rothkopf, Ernest Z. "The Concept of Mathemagenic Activities", *Review of Educational Research,* 40, (June 1970).

22. Robinson F. P. "Study skills for superior students in secondary schools" in Adams, W. Royce, *Increasing Reading Speed* ... op. cit.

23. Berg, Paul C and Rentel, Victor M. "Improving Study Skills", *Journal of Reading,* 9, (April 1966), 343-348.

24. Dechant, Emerald. *Reading Improvement in the Secondary School,* op. cit.

25. Harris, Albert J. *How to Increase Reading Ability,* Fifth Edition, David Macky Company, Inc., New York, 1970 (Fifth Printing, February 1974), pp. 437-38, 447.

26. Dechant, Emerald. *Reading Improvement in the Secondary School,* op. cit.

27. Perry, William G. Jr and Whitlock, Charles P. "The Right to Read Rapidly", *Atlantic Monthly,* 190, (November 1952), 88-96.

28. Weigand, George and Blake, Walter S. Jr. *College Orientation,* Prentice-Hall, Inc., Englewood Cliffs, New Jersey, 1955, p. 39.

29. Smith, Henry P and Dechant, Emerald V. *Psychology in Teaching Reading,* Prentice-Hall International, Inc., London, 1961, p. 339.

30. Dechant, Emerald. *Reading Improvement in the Secondary School* ... op. cit.

31. Robinson, F. P. Study Skills for Superior Students in Secondary Schools, ... op. cit.

32. Robinson, Francis P. *Effects Study,* Rev:ed., Harper and Brothers, Publishers, New York, 1961, p. 50.

33. Stroud, James B. *Psychology in Education,* Longmans, Green and Company, New York, 1956, p. 469.
34. English, H.B; Welborn, E.L and Killian C. D. "Studies in Substance Memorization", *J. gen. Psychol.,* 11, (1934), 233-259.
35. Fry, Edward B. *Reading Instruction for Classroom and Clinic,* McGraw-Hill Book Company, New York, 1972, pp. 435-436.
36. ibid., op. cit.
37. Donald, Sister M. "The SQ3R in Grade Seven", *Journal of Reading,* 11, (October 1967), 33-35, 43.
38. Thomas, Ellen Lamar and Robinson, H. Alan. *Improving Reading in Every Class,* Abridged Edition, Allyn and Bacon, Inc., Boston, 1972 (Fourth Printing, July 1974), pp. 69-134, 71.
39. ibid., op. cit.
40. Pollock, Thomas Clark; Sheridan, Marion C; Hunter, Frances L and Doll, Ronald C. *The Art of Communicating,* Teachers Annotated Edition, The Macmillan Company, New York, 1961, p. 44.
41. Robinson, F. P. *Study Skills for Superior Students ...* op.cit.
42. Dechant, Emerald. *Reading Improving in the Secondary School,* ... op. cit.
43. Eisner, Sigmund and Kermit, Rohde. "Note Making During or After the Lecture", *Journal of Educational Psychology,* 50, (December, 1959), 301-304.
44. Dechant, Emerald. *Reading Improvement in the Secondary School,* ... op. cit.
45. Kollaritsch, Jane. "Organizing Reading for Detailed Learning in a Limited Time" *Journal of Reading,* 13, (October 1969), 29-32.
46. Harris, Albert. *How to Increase Reading Ability,* op. cit.
47. ibid., op. cit.
48. Dechant, Emerald. *Reading Improvement in the Secondary School,* op. cit.
49. ibid.
50. Adler, Mortimer J. "How to Mark a Book", in Adams, W. Royce., *Increasing Reading Speed,* The Macmillan Company, Collier-Macmillan Limited, London, 1969 (Second Printing, 1970), p. 96.
51. Spache, George D and Berg Paul C. *The Art of Efficient Reading,* ... op. cit.
52. Gates, Arthur I. "Developing Higher Levels of Reading Instruction", *Better Readers for our Times,* International Reading Association, Conference Proceedings, Scholastic Magazines, New York, 1956, pp. 95-98.
53. McGeoch, John A and Irion, Arthur L. *The Psychology of Human Learning,* Longmans, Green and Co., New York, 1952, p. 375.
54. Pyle, William H. "Retention as Related to Repetition", *Journal of Educational Psychology*: 2, (1911), 311-321.
55. Tinker, Miles A and McCullough, Constance M. *Teaching Elementary Reading,* Fifth Edition, Prentice-Hall, Inc., Englewood Cliffs, New Jersey, 1975, pp. 226-227.
56. Piekarz, J. A. "Getting Meaning from Reading," *Elementary School Journal,* 56, (1956), 303-809.
57. Tinker, Miles A and McCullough, Constance M. *Teaching Elementary Reading* ... op. cit.

7

A CRITICAL AND CREATIVE APPROACH TO READING

The success of a democracy depends on the ability of the citizens to make choices through a critical analysis of the alternatives before them for selecting their representatives. No doubt literacy is the first condition but it is not enough for making sound judgements. Understanding of literal meanings is just a first layer for the platform of critical reading. A critical reader is a powerful reader. He reads more and in depth. It is only through a critical approach to reading that a person can make sure as to which book is just to be skimmed and which is to be severely read.

The Concept of Critical Reading

Pingry[1] suggests five different emphasis that people have placed on the concept of critical thinking: (1) *Critical thinking* as collecting data, organising data, and formulating hypotheses from data; (2) *Critical thinking* as use of correct principles of logic and understanding the nature of proof; (3) *Critical thinking* as criticism of thinking; (4) *Critical thinking* as related to understanding of the psychology of propaganda and advertising techniques, and (5) *Critical thinking* as synonymous with problem solving.

Simmons[2] remarks that these fi e emphasis in critical thinking or critical reading can be seen clearly in the demands of several content areas of the typical secondary school curriculum. In secondary school

English courses, the student is asked to interpret and analyse various literary selections. In doing so, he must go beyond comprehension of plot and simple character realisation in order to solve the sometimes ambiguously presented problem of symbolic representation of an abstract concept. If he is to escape wild, immaterial, or insignificant interpretation, the student must identify, collect, and synthesise that textural evidence which supports his thematic generalisations. In this quest, he must escape the illogical inference which may be found in the narrative under consideration. This same student is called upon to deal with the most difficult of literary comprehension abilities—that of appreciation. The ability to appreciate imaginative literature, in anything more than the most superficial sense of term, calls for the most sensitive of reactions to the elements of individual word choice, syntax, and broader organisational patterns. Another desired outcome of activities involving appreciation is that the student can integrate his aesthetic reaction to the work of a literary artist to his personal conception of that which is beautiful.

Critical reading is one of the most vital ingredients needed to produce the effective reader. Without this ability, the reader is unable to utilise what is read. The critical reader is one who reacts to the material so that he makes decisions and judgements about it. He must be concerned with such things as the qualifications of the author to write on the topic; the authenticity of the factual information which is presented; the particular biases which were evidenced; and, according to recent revelations, the source of financial support for the writing and publication of the material.[3]

To Helen M. Robinson,[4] critical reading is the judging of the veracity, validity, or worth of what is read, based on sound criteria or standards developed through the reader's previous experiences. To read critically the reader must have an inquiring mind, a knowledgeable background, the ability to suspend judgement until the writer's message is secured, the ability to follow the organisation or logic of the presentation, and an awareness of the author's qualifications and intent concerning what he is saying.

Anderson and Robinson[5] are of the view that critical reading involves three steps. First, the reader must determine what the author is saying. Precisely, he must ferret out the author's "path" of thinking from its beginning or starting point, through its development, its conclusions. Next, in his own mind, he must construct a "model" of the author's path of thinking but with whatever changes his own experience dictates as corrections of the author's ideas. If, in light of his own experience, he sees nothing incongruous in the author's presentation, his critical reading is complete. On the other hand, if his "model" path of thought is different from that of the author, the reader then must compare the ideas and make a decision related to them.

Nila Banton Smith has incisively incorporated the complexity, the demands, and the purpose of critical reading when she says:[6] "In critical reading we need to read with an attitude of inquiry, a desire to seek the truth and a will to search further if necessary. We need to evaluate, challenge, decide upon truthfulness, bias, authenticity. In critical reading the individual needs to react personally in agreeing or disagreeing with the author as a result of personal judgement based upon experience, facts gleaned from various sources, or possibly as a result of clear-cut reasoning."

Critical reading requires a variety of reactions, with one of the most important reactions being his ability to understand what is being communicated. To evaluate the author's purpose, accuracy or implications, the reader must be able to identify facts. The critical reader must examine his source and determine the reliability, accuracy and competence of the author. In addition, the critical reader will learn to identify the author's obvious and hidden assumptions and purposes. He will attempt to distinguish between material representing an opinion and that material backed by facts.[7]

Every bit of reading which a person ever does is a potential source of background understanding for all the reading he will do in the future. "Reading maketh a full man," said Francis Bacon, and he must have meant full of ideas, full of understandings, full of the background for rich comprehension. Any reader's experience can make this clear. He chooses a book or article on some subject with which he is familiar and reads easily with full and deep comprehension. Contrast this experience with what happens when a reader undertakes to read a book in a field in which he has had no background of experience or previous reading. He can make no associations; he probably has no particular purpose except the very general one of getting some ideas about this new field; he misses many of the relationships which are obvious to the sophisticated reader in the field.[8]

Who Is a Critical Reader?

According to Dechant[9]: The good comprehender is a critical reader. He checks the truth, logic reliability, and accuracy of what is written. He looks for contradictory material. He relates the material to his experience. He distinguishes fact from fiction, is concerned with the timeliness of the material and tries to understand the author's motives. The critical reader is as much interested in why something is said as in what is said. He is sensitive to how words are used and is slightly suspicious of the author's biases. He pays particular attention to words with several meanings. He checks the copyright data, the author's reputation, and the publisher's past performance. He looks for the errors of reasoning, of analogy, of overgeneralisation, of oversimplification, and of distortion. He looks for one-sided presentations, biases, faulty inferences, and propaganda. He avoids jumping to quick conclusions.

What constitutes a critical reader? Qaintance[10] presents three characteristics of a critical reader.

First, a critical reader must be biased. Not prejudiced, which he would be if he has formed conclusions without, or in spite of, supporting evidence; but biased, when he has come to a sincere conclusion on the basis of his background of experience with the subject in question. In other words, he must have a stand on the subject under investigation. If he has no stand—we use the term "open mind", though "empty mind" would sometimes be more appropriate—he may accept the first presentation which reaches him, because he lacks sufficient background to dispute the point. At best, he can delay final acceptance of the information pending direct experience or further consultation with other sources.

The second characteristic of a critical reader is his willingness to modify present viewpoint. If a reader is certain that he is right, he will not even consider a change. If he is in error, he is usually unaware of it. Only a critical reader avails himself of opportunities to verify and possibly improve his present fund of information. The person who is always right may not care about the view of someone else. If these other views match his own, his ego is bolstered, but he will explain away or ignore any view that conflicts with his own, because if he were to learn that something else is correct his life would be filled with unbearable contradictions. To avoid such contradictions he must become (pardon the etymological pun) hypocritical.

The third characteristic of a critical reader is that he be willing to involve himself in the consequences of a fact, once he accepts it. In some instances this involves nothing more than going along with the thought of the majority; at other times it may cost him his life and reputation if reading leads him to a personal commitment to action.

In a penetrating essay, "The Critical Reader", Edgar Dale[11] distinguishes between reading the lines, and reading between the lines. He observes, "Reading can be taught as training with fixed limits and predictable responses. Genuine educational experiences, however, have no ceiling, no fixed boundaries, no terminal points."

In all types of critical reading, the reader should make use of his whole background of experiences. Doing so will help him to evaluate whether the new material seems plausible, is only partially correct or appears biased. Sometimes, conflict of the new with past experience may lead to modification or even rejection of the reader's earlier views. There is every possibility that the reader's earlier conclusions may have been based upon incomplete evidence. The reader should always be able to detect propaganda and evaluate critically. Neither slave-like submission nor complete rejection of authority is a healthy sign. A critical reader always thinks for himself. He is neither too receptive nor too suspicious. He demands supporting evidence before making a final judgement so as to resist deceptive forms of propaganda.

Schleich[12] writes: "Only after the reader has ascertained the author's purpose, understood the author's propositions, grasped his ideas and arguments, is he ready to evaluate or react critically to the reading. One of the biggest temptations of the unskilled college reader, or perhaps of any unskilled reader, is the temptation to jump to conclusion—to skip the step of first understanding 'what' the author says, before diagnosing, agreeing or evaluating. Skill in evaluation, therefore, demands first and foremost an attitude of mind—a determination to withhold judgement until the reader has completed the job of analysing and interpreting the material—to give the author the courtesy of hearing him through. In addition, it demands the willingness and the ability of the reader to differentiate between opinion and knowledge. As Francis Bacon (Essay: of Studies) advised, "Read not to contradict and confute, nor to believe and take for granted: nor to find, talk and discourse: but to weigh and consider."

It takes imaginative and intellectual effort to read a book, and facility and achievement grow by exercise. Mortimer J. Adler, in *How to Read a Book,* describes the kind of reading necessary to produce this kind of thinking[13]: "When (people) are in love and are reading a love letter, they read for all they are worth. They read every word three ways: they read between the lines and in the margins, they read the whole in terms of the parts, and each part in terms of the whole; they grow sensitive to context and ambiguity, to insinuation and implication; they perceive the colour of words, the odour of phrases, and the weight of sentences. They may even take punctuation into account. Then, if never before or after, they read."

Critical reading should involve three levels of comprehension:[14]

(*a*) Reading the lines:

What did he say?

(*b*) Reading between the lines:

What did he mean?

(*c*) Reading beyond the lines:

What generalisations may be drawn?

What evaluations may I make?

Steps which might be used in reading critically include[15]: Recognising the author's intent; exploring the scope of the selection;

reflecting about biases, attitudes and other factors in one's own background that may influence one's interpretation of the selection; comprehending accurately what the author said; appraising the soundness of the author's ideas and assumptions: relating and synthesising the ideas presented in the book or article; and applying ideas gained to other material read. To be able to draw accurate conclusions requires thoughtful interpretation and deliberation.

Reading to draw conclusions takes time. After a hypothesis has tentatively been formulated, the reader must test it as he continues his slow, careful, analytical reading. This may require re-reading to verify the hypothesis. With proper guidance pupils can note that in presenting some controversial issues, different authors have arrived at different conclusions. By reading critically, individuals can see bias or prejudice. Some of them may be able to see why the authors arrived at different conclusions creeping into an argument.

A critical reader is always an evaluator—an impartial evaluator. He takes the position of a critic, a judge, a thinker and a philosopher. He is neither an optimist nor a pessimist, he is only an observer—a minute observer. His observation is always objective.

Creative Reading—Is it Different?

Creative reading is the ability which makes it possible for the reader to go beyond the printed lines. It is a prime requisite for intelligent reading. It involves higher mental processes. Creative reading involves the capacity to comprehend something that has meaning away from the written symbols. Hester[16] notes that understanding comes not only of what the author says but also of the reader's response in thought and feeling. This requires the capacity to understand something that has depth: the ability to appreciate that which has beauty, the skill to evaluate controversial material, and the competency to read material in a way which will make words leap from a page and live for the reader.

Critical reading involves judging the quality, accuracy and truthfulness of what is read. It does not end with just reading the lines and getting their implied meanings but involves in itself a severe judgement of the stated facts. Here the final verdict lies with the reader and not with the writer. This verdict may go in favour of the writer or it may even go against the writer within the boundary of the material being read. The reader reacts to the printed material and reads with a critical attitude. DeBoer[17] describes critical reading as involving ... the search for relevant materials, the evaluation of the data, the identification and comparison of sources, and the synthesis of the findings. It involves the capacity for suspended judgement and the interpretation of the writer's motives. But chiefly it involves a sufficient background of knowledge to provide a sound basis for judgement.

Boyd[18] is of the opinion that the critical reader has a propensity to be sceptical, analytical and enquiring. The creative reader has the power of discerning and appreciating that which has beauty, depth and excellence. Thus, creative reading might be viewed as involving new ideas, new insights, and original constructs, and critical reading as reacting to other's ideas or to one's own previous ideas. Before reading critically, one must learn to think creatively because reading itself is a thinking process in this context.

To Russell,[19] critical thinking is comparative and a knowledge of the field is prerequisite.

'Creative reading', on the other hand, is concerned with the production of new ideas, the development of new insights, fresh approaches, and original constructs.[20]

Russell[21] also emphasises that creative thinking involves new ideas, "whereas critical thinking ... involves reaction to other's ideas or to one's own previous ideas. Critical thinking can be creative in that it can produce new insights for the individual, both these insights are concerned with previously established conditions.

A reader who has learned to judge what he reads, both content and manner of presentation, still fails to obtain the greatest pleasure, enjoyment, and even knowledge from his efforts unless, in the doing, he gives something of himself. He must amalgamate the total into his own background of information, what the psychologists call his 'apperceptive mass', and reorganise his ideas to accommodate his new learnings, his new attitudes, or his new feelings. In this reorganisation, he gains new insights— "sees the same things from a different point of view, sees aspects hitherto not noticed, savours the colour and texture of a word or phrase, stores away a new visual image, or feels empathy with characters he has previously ignored or misunderstood".[22]

Emergence of critical and creative reading as distinct functions is fairly recent. Critical reading has long been recognised, categorised, and subskilled. Both critical reading and creative reading are built on the basic reading skills. Although some experts tend to combine critical and creative reading under a single label such as receptive or stimulative reading, most authorities recognise the additive qualities of these levels; that is, the virtual impossibility of attaining the higher levels of reading without mastery of reading entry through word identification and word meaning and literal, interpretive, and analytical reading of the content, all of which assume a thorough grasp of the author's intent in his writing. Whereas there has been a fair amount of research on critical reading, the research on creative reading is meagre. Both, however, are founded on the assumption that reading is thinking and that critical and creative reading must be even more intimately related to critical and creative thinking.[23]

Some thirty years ago, Edgar Dale beautifully simplified the total task of reading from the basic to the most complex, from the literal to the creative. His three steps, as true today as then, are:[24]

1. Reading the lines, the job of getting the simplest sense of what the writer says;
2. Reading between the lines, discovering what the author meant to say, which is critical reading; and
3. Reading beyond the lines, judging and interpreting what is read in the light of one's own problems; one's own experiences—a task which is creative reading.

All of this, he recommends, can be accomplished through questioning and questioning attitudes.

To become a critical reader, one requires (*a*) competence in basic skills and abilities in word perception and comprehension, (*b*) an enquiring attitude, (*c*) a background of information about the topic, (*d*) ability to weigh evidence while suspending judgement, and (*e*) control of emotional reactions or prejudice regarding the author or material.

Many adults never learn to read analytically and hence never learn to deal successfully with materials with which they disagree. They allow their negative reactions to the author—his nationality, race, religion or viewpoint—to pervert their comprehension of his reading. Other readers are impressed by the writer's reputation or name and thus are led to accept his implications without first examining the facts. This is absolutely wrong. One must only be concerned with the viewpoints of the author. A critical reader is like an impartial judge whose duty is to give judgement. After all why should he be concerned with other variables. A critical reader uses his brain beyond his emotions and feelings. A creative reader goes one step ahead when he presents more of himself for getting the routine solutions to the problems. He gives newness to his reading approaches in creative reading. Thought to be the highest and most challengeable of all mental process, it occurs when the reader with the writer creates a novel idea or visualises a different, a unique relationship.

SUMMARY

Critical reading is one of the most vital ingredients needed to produce the effective reader. In all types of critical reading, the reader makes use of his whole background of experiences. This helps him evaluate the authenticity of the material. Critical reading involves judging the quality, accuracy and truthfulness of what is being read. It does not end with just reading the lines and getting their literal meaning, but involves in itself a severe judgement of the stated facts. Here, the final verdict lies with the reader and not with the writer. The verdict may go in favour of the writer or it may even go against the writer within the boundary of the material read. The reader reacts to the printed material and reads with a critical attitude. Creative reading involves the capacity to comprehend something that has meaning away from the written symbols. It is concerned with the production of new ideas, the development of new insights, fresh approaches and original contributions. A critical reader is like an impartial judge whose duty is to give judgement. A critical reader uses his brain beyond his emotions and feelings. A creative reader goes one step ahead when he presents more of himself for getting the routine solutions to problems. Creative reading is considered the most challengeable of all mental processes where the reader gives newness to his reading approaches.

REFERENCES

1. Pingry, Robert E. "Critical Reading—What is it?" *The Mathematics Teacher,* (November 1951), 466-67.
2. Simmons, John S. "Reasoning Through Reading", *Journal of Reading,* 8, (April 1965), 311-314.
3. McCord, Carol S. "Developing an Effective Reader: Secondary", in Dorothy M. Dietrich and Virginia H. Mathews (Eds.), *Development of Lifetime Reading Habits,* IRA, Newark, Delaware 19711, 1968, pp. 26-27.
4. Robinson, Helen M. "Developing Critical Readers", in Russell G. Stauffer (Ed.), *Dimensions of Critical Reading,* Proceedings of the Reading Conference, University of Delaware, 1964, pp. 1-2.
5. Anderson, Oliver and Robinson, Alan H. "Reading Comprehension", in Marion D. Jenkinson (Ed.), *Reading Instruction: An International Forum,* Proceedings of the First World Congress on Reading held at UNESCO House, Paris, France, August 8-9, 1966, IRA, Newark, Delaware 19711, 1967, p. 107.
6. Smith, Nila Banton. *Reading Instruction for Today's Children,* Prentice-Hall, Englewood Cliffs, New Jersey, 1963, p. 270.
7. Tobin, Richard L. "Reading is a Habit", *Saturday Review,* (April 8, 1961), 51-52.
8. Niles, Olive S. "Comprehension Skills", *The Reading Teacher,* 17, (September 1963), 2-7.
9. Dechant, Emerald. *Reading Improvement in the Secondary School,* Prentice Hall, Inc., Englewood Cliffs, New Jersey, 1973, p. 268.
10. Qaintance, William J. (Brother). "Critical Reader—As If There's Any Other Kind", *The Reading Teacher,* 20 (October 1966), 49-53.
11. Dale, Edgar. "The Critical Reader", *Ohio State News Letter,* 30 (4), (January 1965).
12. Schleich, Miriam. "Sequential Reading Skills at the College Level", *Reading and Inquiry,* IRA Proceedings, 10, (1965), 39-42.
13. Adler, Mortimer J. *How to Read a Book,* Simon and Schuster, Inc., New York, 1956, p. 14.
14. Cutter, Virginia. "And Beyond the Lines", in *Vistas in Reading,* IRA Proceeding, 11, Part 1, (1966), 64-68.
15. Boyd, Gertrude A. *Teaching Communication Skills in the Elementary School,* Van Nostrand Reinhold Company, New York, 1970, pp. 313&32.
16. Hester, Kathleen B. "Creative Reading: A Neglected Area", *Education,* 79, (1959), 537-541.
17. DeBoer, John. "Teaching Critical Reading", *Elementary English,* 23, (1964), 68-72.
18. Boyd, Gertrude A. Teaching Communication Skills in elementary School, op cit.

19. Russell, David. *Children's Thinking,* Ginn and Company, Boston, 1956, pp. 283 & 306.

20. Huus, Helen. "Critical and Creative Reading", in *Reading and Inquiry,* IRA Proceedings, 10, (1965), 115-117.

21. Russell, David. *Children's Thinking,* op. cit.

22. Huss, Helen. "Critical and Creative Reading", op. cit.

23. Courtney, Leonard (Brother). "Critical and Creative Reading in the Secondary Schools", in Dorothy M. Dietrich and Virginia H. Mathews (Eds.), *Development of Lifetime Reading Habits,* IRA, Newark, Delaware 19711, 1968, p. 32.

24. Dale, Edgar. "The Art of Reading", *The News Letter,* The Ohio State University, Columbus (Feb. 1946).

8

DEVELOPMENT OF RATE IMPROVEMENT PROGRAMMES

Introduction

Almost a century ago, people used to think that a reader perceives words letter by letter. The whole methodology of teaching beginning reading was based on the assumption that a person looks at each separate letter as he reads. Even up to this day we teach our children in schools beginning with isolated alphabets.

It was in the year 1879 when Professor Javal of Paris University became interested in studying the eye movements. To begin with, he tried to observe the eyes of the people who were reading by just looking at them with his own naked eyes. As the eyes of the readers moved very fleetingly, Javal could not tell what took place. Javal did not get discouraged. He again tried placing a mirror in front of the reader, watching the reader's eye in the mirror. But this also did not work. He thought of taking help from his friends but all in vain. Nobody realised his difficulty to invent some way of checking the eye movements of a person engaged in reading. "Nonsense", they said, "why bother about something that everybody already knows? The eyes have to look at each letter in every word as they move across a line of print. Otherwise, how could the reader tell one word from another?" Javal, however, doubted if a person recognised printed sentences letter by letter, so he kept busy in figuring out some method by which he could detect the way in which the human eye works when one reads.

Javal fashioned a cup of plaster of Paris which was to fit over the eyeball of the person reading. He also made a small hole (an aperture) in the middle of the cup through which the reading material could be seen. While the plaster of Paris was still damp and pliable, Javal inserted a very thin and light stick into the outer side of the cup. When the cup dried, the stick was securely rooted in the plaster of Paris. He also smoked a drumhead. The smoke left a heavy black coating on the drumhead. When the plaster of Paris cup with a stick and the smoked drumhead were ready, Javal asked a man to sit close to the drumhead and read. The plaster of Paris cup was placed over one eye of the man, and as he read, the stick traced a design in the smoke coating on the drumhead. This design revealed that the eyes did not look at one letter at a time or even at one word at a time. Rather, they proceeded in a series of pauses and jerks, stopping only three or four times in covering an entire line.

A few years later, Ahrens (1891) and Huey (1906) improved upon the plaster of Paris cup. In that they used an ivory cup to which they attached a bristle. The bristle recorded the eye movements on a smoked drumhead. Other investigators began to make studies of their own using different kinds of equipment. Finally, a huge camera was designed by a professor who devoted a year's time to its perfection and it cost 6000 dollars.

Emergence of New Methodology in Rapid Reading

Once a scientific procedure for detecting eye movements was developed, hundreds of studies were made with all kinds of readers at various age levels showing decided differences between the way poor readers read and the way good readers pursue the printed page. These studies revealed that the poor reader perceives just one word or perhaps a part of word while a good reader takes in group of words at one seeing. It is evident and researches in the area have proved that the person who takes in an entire group of words at one seeing can read more rapidly than one whose eyes fixate on one word at a time or perhaps on parts of words. From this concept emerged a new methodology in rapid reading.

Romanes early experiments on the problems, getting "practised readers" to read paragraphs in a book containing "simple statements of simple facts", and noting the time needed for the reading. The moment the reading ceased, the reader wrote down all that could be remembered of what was read. Romanes found "astonishing differences in the rate of reading". "The differences may amount to 4 to 1; or, otherwise stated, one individual may be able in a given time to read four times as fast as another. Moreover, it appeared that there was no relationship between slowness of reading and power of assimilation."

Miss Adelaide M. Abell, in the *Educational Review* for October, 1894, reported experiments on the reading rate of forty Wellesley College girls, the work being done under the direction of Professor Calkins. She found that, on the whole, swift reading saves time without necessarily decreasing comprehension. She believes that the rate will be increased by "increasing the rapidity of association, by repeating and multiplying associations, and by intensifying interest and attention." She concludes that although every individual probably has his maximum rate, "determined by his natural quickness of comprehension and association, it is yet possible and desirable to some extent to increase the ordinary rate."

Dr J. O. Quantz tested fifty university students, juniors and seniors of the University of Wisconsin, to determine their normal and maximal rates in reading, and experimented upon them further to determine the factors and conditions upon which rate of reading depended. He found that his readers varied from 210 words per minute for the slowest to 528 words per minute for the fastest, when reading at normal speed. At maximal speed the rate ranged from 210 words per minute to 732 words. Generally, those who read fast at normal speed excelled in the maximal tests, and the slow readers were generally slow in both.

In testing the ability to reproduce what was read, he found that the rapid readers were on an average about 37 per cent superior to the slow reader in the quality of their work. "The superiority of the rapid reader is also shown by the fact that his memory of the substance of his reading is more exact than that of the slow reader."

Dr Quantz found that persons who are of the visual type "are slightly more rapid readers than the auditory type." Quickness of visual perception, shown in rapid recognition of colours, words, geometrical forms such as circles, squares, diamonds, etc., was found to be "an important factor in deciding one's rate of reading." Considering all the factors which he found to contribute to rapid reading are, "order of importance, visual perception, practice in reading from childhood on, power of concentration, mental alertness estimated by rapidity of original composition, scholarly ability as decided by college records". These results were found in general for the readers tested, and as a particular confirmation the person whose reading was by far the most rapid of all those excelled markedly in practically all the above conditions of rapid reading. It is interesting to note that the judgements of readers about themselves, as to whether they are slow, medium, or fast readers, agreed very well with the results of Dr Quantz's tests of speed as taken later.

Dearborn tested the reading rate of a considerable number of readers, and found that for a given class of reading matter the fastest reader read more than three times as fast as the slowest. He also carefully tested the reading rates of three graduate students, one a mathematician, one a teacher in a secondary school, and one a psychologist, for various classes of reading matter selected from literature and science. Each of these persons had quite different rates for the different classes of matter read. However, the fastest reader in his most interesting subject, in this case the mathematician, read much the fastest in all the classes of matter, the secondary teacher read much more slowly than the mathematician in all the classes, and the psychologist read much more slowly still in all but one class. Dearborn draws from this data the conclusion "that one who reads rapidly in a given style and class of subject-matter will read somewhat proportionally faster than a slow reader, whatever, within certain recognised limits, the nature of the style and subject-matter."

After the reading of a passage in the reader's usual way, Dearborn had him read it again "as rapidly as possible consistent with getting the sense." The reader believed that he 'usually' read at his maximum rate, and that this was particularly true of his first reading of this passage, the matter being especially interesting. It was found, however, that in the second reading nearly one-third of the total time was saved, the absolute time of nearly every pause being diminished, fewer pauses being made, and "the average distance of the eye's first pause from the left edge of the page noticeably increased." The length of the 'initial' fixations in the lines were, however, even a little longer than before, permitting the preliminary general survey of the line which Dearborn finds to be needful for the more rapid reading. He finds, indeed, the "rapidity of reading is not necessarily correlated with regularity of movement", some of the fastest and slowest readers being found equally regular in movement. But "a wider 'spanning' of attention", shown in the frequency of long pauses at the line's beginning and in the fewer fixations per line, is found to be characteristic of the more rapid readers. "The slow readers have a narrower span or working extent of attention, and a greater total arc of movement."

Huey[1] is of the opinion that there can usually be much improvement in the rate of reading. There seems to be a rhythm into which each reader ordinarily falls in ordinary reading, and it seems doubtful whether ordinary practice changes this rhythm after it is well established. Doubtless many of us dawdle along in our reading at a plodding pace which was set and hardened in days of listless poring over uninteresting tasks, or in imitation of the slow reading aloud which was so usually going on either with ourselves or with others in the school.

Growth of Interest in Increasing Speed of Reading

Interest in increasing speed of reading was evident in professional literature as early as the period 1920-1930 when studies showed the possibilities of improving speed of reading in relatively short periods of time with gains in comprehension.[2] For example, as early as 1921, John A. O' Brien described the efficiency of a reading improvement programme for pupils in grades 3-8.[3] During a short training period, he succeeded in eliciting a 56 per cent gain in speed of reading and a small gain, too, in comprehension.

From 1925-1930, attempts were made to improve rate and comprehension in college classes.

Even before the war a number of colleges and universities—Harvard, Dartmouth, Columbia, Minnesota, and others—had instituted reading courses or clinics, but these were usually reserved for freshmen or for upper classmen whose academic difficulties appeared to stem from poor reading. Very few non-students were accepted. However, when the Adult Reading Clinic at the University of Chicago began operating in 1941, it was opened to students and non-students alike.[4] In the six years of its existence Dr Guy Buswell worked with 1500 adults and demonstrated that it is possible to secure a material increase in rate without sacrificing comprehension.

Gilbert[5] writes:

"With the growth in interest in adult reading, certain investigators were curious about a particular question; they wanted to know whether it was possible to increase speed without loss of comprehension. In order to find the answer, they selected individuals with adequate comprehension, trained them with speed techniques and measured the results. They found that speed can be increased without loss of comprehension; they also found that speed training alone does not improve comprehension.

"It is important to note that in these experiments the scientists were not concerned with building total effectiveness in reading, nor with the diversified problems of adult readers. They were interested in just one question, and they carefully selected for their experiments only those people with adequate initial comprehension."

The first adult instruction was largely remedial in character: it was intended for those with serious reading handicaps. Today's instruction is more often developmental than remedial; it is designed for the average readers and the good readers who feel the importance of becoming superior readers. It is based upon the thesis that few read to capacity, no matter how good they are. There is mounting evidence to show that good readers gain more through training than do poor readers.[6]

Rapid Reading Gains Universal Appeal

The dollars and cents value of good reading has appealed to business people. They look at it this way: if a man with an annual salary of 20,000 dollars spends two hours per day on business reading, the cost amounts to about 5000 dollars a year. If he can be trained to do the same reading equally well in half the time, the cost is reduced by one-half and he saves 2500 dollars. Banks, department stores, manufacturing concerns, chemical companies and other commercial establishments over the country are introducing improvement courses for their personnel—particularly for their executives. There is a constantly increasing flow of mature adults in different reading situations who are interested in self-improvement.[7]

Advocates of rate improvement programmes claim that such programmes may also lead to more accurate perception, more accurate and more rapid visual discrimination, wider span of apprehension and of perception, better attention and concentration, shorter reaction time, fewer regressions, decrease in the number and duration of fixations, reduction of vocalisation, better comprehension, and general improvement in perceptual skills.[8]

Appraisal of Rate Improvement Programmes

Within the past few years numerous reports have appeared describing the phenomenally high speeds achieved by students of speed-reading training programmes. Reading rates ranging from 2000 to 8000 words per minute are often reported. One newspaper article told of an individual reading at 30,000 words per minute. Information of this nature is being disseminated by various journals, magazines, brochures and circulars, with radio and television joining the chorus. We often hear people speak of other reading feats, these being performed by mental giants, who are capable of reading a page at a glance and those, with a more limited span, grasp complete paragraphs with a single fixation. Since these reports are being circulated, it would seem desirable to conduct scientific enquiry concerning their validity.[9]

Mrs Evelyn Wood contacted scores of people in all parts of the nation (USA) who read at 1500 words or so a minute and studied their habits. "They all read straight down the page" she told the USF (University South Florida) audience, and they told her they saw whole groups of words, groups totalling as much as half a page at a time.[10]

A 12 week study session, Mrs Wood said, with two hours of class work weekly and another hour a day in practice can bring average reading speeds between 2000 and 3000 words a minute with full comprehension.[11]

The operators of this particular speed-reading system called reading dynamics say they do not feel satisfied if their pupils are reading fewer than 1000 to 2500 words a minute at the end of the twelve-week course. If a student is particularly adept and does his homework—at least an hour a day he may, it is claimed, come to read 6000 or more words a minute. The pace of the average graduate is 350 words. But if you let your eye sweep over it, say from top to bottom, you grasp the idea of it quickly. So you turn the pages with your left hand and run your right hand down them with a gently caressing motion letting your eye follow the right hand from top to bottom instead of reading across the lines from left to right.[12]

During the past few years, claims for phenomenally rapid rates of reading have repeatedly appeared in current publications. For example, in the '*Wall Street Journal*', September 27, 1967, it was noted by Ira West that:

"... Evelyn Wood ... who founded the chain of speed-reading schools in Washington, D.C., in 1959 argues that even though the average person reads at a rate of about 250 words a minute, maximum reading speed limits don't exist. Mrs Wood claims that some people can read more than 40,000 words a minute—a speed that would enable them, to knock off 'Gone With the Wind' in 12 minutes."[13]

A novel method described by Ira West[14], which is employed by Evelyn Wood and her associates "is designed to replace the average person's word by word, line by line reading pattern." The method ... is to expand the student's reading vision so his eye sees large areas of print and to require him to read a printed page at such a high speed that he breaks the habit of "sub-vocalising", or hearing every word mentally.

In this approach:

A student is taught to move a finger down a page in rapid, zigzag patterns and force his eyes to keep pace by taking in large groups of words at a glance ... This technique ... enables graduates to read at least 1000 to 3000 words a minute without skipping or skimming.

A clear description of the improvement of reading by the Wood approach is found in Russell G. Stauffer's account of the introduction to this procedure at the University of Delaware.[15] Stauffer, himself, took the course. He states that he "checked in at an initial rate of about 750 words per minute and checked out reading at about 5000 words per minute." Stauffer discussed carefully certain features of the approach and reports that in a similar class later set up for his colleagues, "the men progressed at varying rates; three of them did unusually well, attaining rates of 4000-5000 words per minute reading fiction and rates of about 2500-3000 words per minute reading non-fiction."

The claims related to increasing reading speed made by Evelyn Wood Reading Dynamics are most widely known in the rapid reading world. Their advertisements[16] claim, among other things, to "at least triple your present reading efficiency or your tuition will be refunded." The course consists of eight 2½ hour sessions, one session each week, and the average "student reads 4.7 times faster than his starting speed with equal or better comprehension." Their advertisements further state that "conventional rapid reading courses aspire to 450-600 words per minute. Most Reading Dynamics graduates can read between 1500 and 3000 words per minute, and many go even higher."

The essence of Panoramic Reading, a speed and remedial reading programme of Vearl G. McBride, is presented in the January 14, 1968 issue of the Quincy, Illinois, *Herald-Whig.*[17] McBride says that his students are not skimming but are "... seeing all of the words and understanding them." He emphasises the need to consider individual differences in teaching speed-reading and recommends an eleven-step approach which includes holding the book at different angles "to determine which angle is best for you", practising seeing words fast, "with no comprehension or as little as you can manage, for four to six hours", and then "gradually increase your comprehension and maintain the best speed you can".

People who wish to read faster than 3000 words a minute can enrol in the Optimation Rapid Reading Course, which has since been taken over by the Rapid Reading Foundation[18] of Chicago. "Most Optimation students, from children to senior citizens, learn to read at the rate of 5000 words per minute" an advertisement[19] claims. "Many are able to read 10,000 words per minute—or more. One 20-year-old university student from Chicago learned to read at the incredible pace of 40,000 words per minute with increased comprehension!"

In the November 1960 issue of *The Reading Teacher,* Stauffer[20] referred to the Wood Reading Dynamics Method as a "magnificent ambition". Commenting on this Spache[21], citing Stauffer's phrase questioned the veracity of the claims of the Reading Dynamics Programme and remarked: ... assuming that the reader can recognise and comprehend the maximum span of three words per fixation, and that there are no regressions, the line of ten words is read in .66 of a second, or at a rate of approximately fifteen words per second or nine hundred words per minute. Any speed greater than this involves omitting lines, the technique recognised by most authorities as skimming, not "reading". It is apparent that the upper speeds suggested as feasible in these various newspaper articles are not possible in the act of reading as here defined, but must be characteristic of such performances as skimming or scanning, in which relatively large portions of the reading material are skipped.

Disputing the article "Is This a Breakthrough in Reading?" by George D. Spache which appeared in January 1962 issue of *The Reading Teacher,* Stevens and Reginald[22] claim that rapid readers can read routine material faster than 1500 words per minute, but they must have a conceptual background in the material. In addition, the writers claim that fast readers are able to break the sound barrier and move directly from symbol to meaning.

Morton[23] found that readers shortened reading time or increased speed by using greater contextual constraints. Fast readers tend to use contextual clues more efficiently. In effect, they see fewer words when reading.

Stauffer[24] also claims that it is possible for some people to eventually read almost as fast as they think; first, though, they must break the "oral-visual" barrier.

In an article which appeared in March 1969, G. Jarry McLaughlin[25] points out that Spache "identifies reading as 'having every word in clear vision'." Thus, it would appear "that we can see only three words every fifth of a second" or about 900 words per minute. These words "are seen with greater than 50 per cent acuity" according to Spache. McLaughlin suggests "that speed-reading may be explained by parallel processing, that is by simultaneously decoding fragments of several sentences seen in peripheral vision" defined as what can be seen "with 50 per cent acuity or less."

Three years later, this fledgling research emerged as a doctoral dissertation in which Liddle[26] found that students taught by the Wood method increased their reading rate but "an analysis of the data ... does not substantiate the claim that exceptional rates are obtained without a loss in comprehension."

Similar findings were obtained by Taylor[27] who tested 41 graduates of the Reading Dynamics programme and found that their comprehension level was 45 per cent on a test composed of true-false items.

Rovin[28] in a study involving high school students, and Thalberg Eller[29], in another investigation, also found that the Reading Dynamics programme produced rate gains but lower comprehension when compared with other methods. On the other hand, Adams[30], in an article entitled "The phenomenon of Supernormal Reading Ability", cites twelve students who read over 1500 words a minute with comprehension at 70 per cent or more on the Diagnostic Reading Test. He further suggests that satisfactory comprehension may be obtained at "ultra-high reading speed".[31]

Additional views on aspects of the Wood Method are presented by Wheeler, and Wheeler[32] who write that "when thinking is unrestricted by excessive verbalising, it is possible to read at rates of thousands of words a minute."

... It is rare, that a student learns to read easy material more rapidly than a thousand words a minute. Even doubling or trebling one's speed of reading easy material with an accompanying proportionate increase in study-type rate results in ease and comfort in reading for pleasure which in turn tends to increase rate in accord with the individual's general tempo. There is no magic about the techniques used. The major teaching procedure involves high motivation and continuous encouragement ... [33]

Paul Witty and associates[34] report:

Rare indeed was the student who obtained a higher rate than 800-900 words per minute during courses designed to improve reading rate and comprehension. However, the average student did improve greatly in reading the types of materials introduced. For example, for 180 students: the average rate (for relatively easy materials) at the beginning of the programme was 272 words per minute. After the programme was completed, the students read the same type of materials at an average rate of 474 words per minute. Moreover, the students learned to "skim" some materials, to read others carefully in terms of certain purposes, and to apply study skills intensively in others. It was recognised that different rates of reading should be anticipated as students read different kinds of materials for different purposes. Accordingly, rate of reading was not looked upon as a single ability which characterised all of a pupil's reading, but as an aggregate of different rates.

Taylor[35] observed that "through hundreds of studies involving eye-movement photography, it has been determined that no one has an average span that permits the intake of a phrase at a fixation. The EDL eye-movement photography study to establish norms for reading performance shows that the average span for the college student reading 280 words per minute is only 1.1 words." In another study involving the photographing of the eye movements of graduates of the Reading Dynamics Institute, Taylor noted that no difference existed between those who did and those who did not take the Wood programme. Mrs Wood, however replies that existing eye cameras are not sophisticated enough to record her students' reading patterns.[36]

Evelyn Wood[37] explains that "the Reading Dynamics method is a process of reading down the page, rather than across each line, using the hand as a pacer. The aim is 'visual reading' with virtual elimination of subvocal speech. Readers who have to 'hear' as well as see words never read very fast because they slow down to listen."

Continuing, she writes, "The first problem, then is learning how to let words and ideas come into the mind faster, and the second is learning how to get meaning from words and ideas without relying on 'inner speech'. The single word is no more important to the total understanding of what is read than the single film frame passing through the projector is to the understanding of the motion picture. As hundreds of single frames pass through a projector much faster than each single frame could be individually projected, they give the viewer the feeling, atmosphere, and detail of an entire film. Similarly, dynamic reading enables the reader to see a story much as the author thought it through."

In the 1968 Yearbook of the National Society for the Study of Education, Huus[38] writes:

It is difficult to make evaluations of speed-reading because of the variation in the level of difficulty of the materials, the format in which the material is presented, the motivation and purposes for reading, the quality of the comprehension questions used, the standards of comprehension accepted, and the background of the subjects. There is a place for rapid reading and also for skimming, but the two are not synonymous. The research to date does not discriminate sufficiently between them. Furthermore, follow-up studies to determine permanency of gains have not been reported; therefore, until more information is available, claims of fantastic gains must be viewed cautiously.

Conclusion

A carefully planned rapid reading programme, taking individual differences into consideration, providing for drill in the mechanics of reading and for the development of needed comprehension skills, and encouraging recreational reading, results in producing efficient readers who are better equipped to take their place in the society. Such a programme should never be restricted to poor readers alone. If drill in mechanics and in comprehension skills aids poor readers, good readers benefit to even greater degree. An efficient reader is always an interested reader. He extracts joy out of the reading activity and rightly so because the product of efficient reading habits is interest, rather than interest being the sole foundation of good reading habits. In the beginning stages, we learn to read but afterwards we read to learn. Similarly in the initial stages if we show our interest for efficient reading, afterwards efficient reading results in creating interests.

It is not a matter of disgrace to any adult to suggest that he can improve his own reading. Nearly everyone needs some improvement and many need a great deal.

Usually a student who applies himself in a development reading class can double or triple his reading rates with different types of material. For instance, an average student or adult reading at the average speed of about 250 wpm can expect to increase his rates to 500 or 700 wpm with some materials. The student learns to read faster because he learns to overcome all of the barriers that have kept him from reading at faster rates. He learns to read word groups rather than one or two words at a glance. He learns to overcome lip movement and the sounding out of words in his head as he reads. He learns to overcome faulty eye movements and regression tendencies that slow him down. He learns to develop a faster, more flexible vocabulary. But most of all, he learns how to develop his powers of comprehension and to understand better what he is reading. The development of all these skills ultimately makes him a better and faster reader.[39]

The challenge of knowledge explosion demands efficient readers. Estimates indicate that it took approximately 1750 years for the first doubling of knowledge, 150 years for the second doubling, 50 years for the third, and only 10 years for the fourth. The fifth doubling may take 5 or even less years. Should we not then take the advantage of speed-reading programmes which seem to meet the challenge of time?

SUMMARY

Earlier experiments by Javal, Ahrens and Huey showed decided differences between the way poor readers read and the way good readers pursue the printed page. These experiments revealed that the poor reader perceives just one word or perhaps a part of word while a good reader takes in a group of words at one seeing. From this concept emerged a new methodology in rapid reading. Abell's experiment with college girls concluded that although every individual probably has his maximum rate, "determined by his natural quickness of comprehension and association, it is yet possible and desirable to some extent to increase the ordinary rate." Quantaz found that persons who are of the visual type "are slightly more rapid readers than the auditory type." Dearborn found that for a given class of reading matter the fastest reader read more than three times as fast as the slowest.

Interest in increasing speed of reading was evident in the professional literature as early as the period 1920-1930, when studies showed the possibilities of improving speed of reading in relatively short periods of time with gains in comprehension Buswell worked with 1500 adults and demonstrated that it is possible to secure a material increase in rate without sacrificing comprehension. Within the past few years numerous reports have appeared describing phenomenally high speeds achieved by students of speed-reading programmes. Wood, McBride, Stauffer, Wheeler and Wheeler are still working in the area of speed-reading following different approaches for rate gains. Spache and Witty are of the view that reading speeds beyond 800 and 900 words per minute do not come under the purview of individual's physiological perceptual limits. Adams claims that a student who attends a developmental reading course can double or triple his reading speed with different types of materials. The student learns to read faster because he learns to overcome all of the barriers that have kept him from reading at faster rates.

REFERENCES

1. Huey, Edmund Burke. *The Psychology and Pedagogy of Reading,* (The Macmillan Co., New York, 1908), The M.I.T. Press, Cambridge, 1968, pp. 170-179.
2. Witty, Paul A. "Evaluation of Methods and Devices to Improve Reading Rate and Comprehension", *Elementary English,* 31, (May 1954).

3. O'Brien, John A. *Silent Reading,* The Macmillan Company, New York, 1921.

4. Buswell, Guy T. "The Improvement of Rate and Comprehension in Reading", in *Adapting Reading Programmes to Wartime Needs,* Supplementary Educational Monographs, Number 57, University of Chicago Press, Chicago, 1943, pp. 248-252.

5. Gilbert, Doris W. *Power and Speed in Reading,* Prentice-Hall, Inc., Englewood Cliffs, N.J., 1956 (Tenth Printing, May 1964), pp. 107, 109.

6. ibid, op. cit.

7. Gilbert, Doris W. *Power and Speed in Reading,* op. cit.

8. Dechant, Emerald. *Reading Improvement in the Elementary School,* Prentice-Hall, Inc., Englewood Cliffs, New Jersey, 1973, p. 320.

9. Walton, Howard N in Lawrence E. Hafner, *Improving Reading in Secondary Schools,* The Macmillan Company, New York, 1967, p. 277.

10. "Ten Times Present Speeds—Specialist at University South Florida Teases Professors with Promise of High Speed Reading", *Tampa Tribuue,* March 26, 1961.

11. Spache, George D. "Is this a Breakthrough in Reading?" *Reading Teacher,* 15, (January 1962), 259-263.

12. Twelve Lawmakers Go to Reading Class", *New York Times,* Sunday June 11, 1961.

13. Witty, Paul A. "Rate of Reading—A Crucial Issue", *Journal of Reading.* 13(2), (November 1969), p. 102.

14. West, Ira. "Evelyn, Wood Schools" Speed-Reading Claim's Spark a Controversy", *The Wall Street Journal,* (September 27, 1967).

15. Stauffer, Russell G. "Speed Reading at the University of Delaware", *Speed Reading: Practices and Procedures,* Vol. 10, Proceedings of the 44th Annual Education Conference held at the University of Delaware, March 2-3, 1962. Compiled and edited by Russell G. Stauffer, The Reading-Study Center, School of Education, University of Delaware, Newark, Delaware, 1963.

16. *The New York Times Magazines,* January 8, 1967, p. 65.

17. Bender, Craig. "C-S Professor's Methods Develop Top Reading Speeds", Quincy, Illinois: *Herald-Whig,* January 14, 1968.

18. Ayres, Robert B. *Letter,* February 12, 1968, *Rapid Reading Foundation,* 10 North Clark Street, Chicago, Illinois 60602.

19. *Chicago Tribune,* January 1, 1967.

20. Stauffer, Russell G. "A Magnificent Ambition", *Reading Teacher* 14 (November 1960), 74, 92.

21. Spache, George D. "Is this a Breakthrough in Reading?" *Reading Teacher,* op. cit.

22. Stevens, George L and Reginald, Orem. "Characteristic Reading Techniques of Rapid Readers", *Reading Teacher,* 17 (November 1963), 102-108.

23. Morton, John. "The Effects of Context Upon Speed Reading, Eye Movement and Eye-Voice Span", *Quarterly Journal of Experimental Psychology,* 16, (1964), 340-354.

24. Stauffer, Russell G. "Speed Reading Versatility", in J. Allen Figurel, (ed.), *Challenge and Experiment in Reading,* Proceedings of the International Reading Associations, Scholastic Magazines, New York, Vol. 7, 1962, pp. 206-210.

25. McLaughlin, G. Harry. "Reading at 'impossible' Speeds", *Journal of Reading,* 12, (March 1969).

26. Liddle, William. "An Initial Investigation of the Wood Reading Dynamics Method", Doctoral Dissertation, University of Delaware, 1965.

27. Taylor, Stanford E. "An Evaluation of Forty-One Trainees Who Had Recently Completed the Reading Dynamics Programme", *Problems, Programmes, and Projects in College-Adult Reading,* Eleventh Yearbook of the National Reading Conference, National Reading Conference, Milwaukee., 1962.

28. Rovin, Ronald. "The Effectiveness of Teaching Speed Reading to Underachieving and Volunteer Students", Unpublished paper involving a study in three high schools in a northwest Chicago suburban community, August 1967.

29. Eller, Thalberg and William, Stanton P. "A Comparison of two Widely Differing Methods of Teaching Reading Efficiency", *New Developments in Programmes and Procedures for College-Adult Reading,* Twelfth Yearbook of the National Reading Conference, National Reading Conference, Milwaukee., 163, 112-123.

30. Adams, R. Buchanan. "The phenomenon of Supernormal Reading Ability", *New Developments in Programmes and Procedures for College-Adult Reading,* Twelfth Yearbook of the National Reading Conference, National Reading Conference, Milwaukee, 1963, pp. 133-142.

31. Adams, R. Buchanan. "Reading Comprehension and Reading Speed: A Discussion of Research", *Reading as an Intellectual Activity,* Proceedings of the International Reading Association, 8, 1963, pp. 241-243.

32. Wheeler, Lester R and Wheeler, Viola D. "A New Era in Reading", *Reading Teacher,* 16, (November 1962), 109-112.

33. Robinson, Helen M and Smith, Helen K. "Rate Problems in the Reading Clinic", *The Reading Teacher,* 15, (May 1962).

34. Witty, Paul A; Stolarz, Theodore and Cooper, William. "Some Results of a Remedial Reading Programme for College Students", *School and Society,* 76, (December 13, 1952).

35. Taylor, Stanford E. "An Evaluation of Forty-one Trainees Who Had Presently Completed the Reading Dynamics Programme"... op. cit.

36. Hermann, Robert. "The Argument Over Racing Through Printing: Is it Speed You Need to Enjoy Reading?" *The National Observer,* Reprinted in Ralph C. Staiger and David A. Sohn (Ed.), *New Directions in Reading,* Bantam Books, New York, 1967, 147-155.

37. Wood, Evelyn N. "Opinions Differ on Speed Reading", *NEA Journal,* 52, (April 1983), 44-46.

38. Huus, Helen. "Innovations in Reading Instruction: At Later Levels", *Innovation and Change in Reading Instruction,* Sixty-Seventh Yearbook of the National Society for the Study of Education, University of Chicago Press, Chicago., 1968.

39. Adams, W. Royce. *Increasing Reading Speed,* The Macmillan Company, Collier-Macmillan Limited, London, 1969 (Second Printing, 1970), p. 3.

9

MECHANICAL DEVICES FOR RATE IMPROVEMENT

It is a matter of general experience that very often a person can read faster, but he has developed a habit of moving slowly. He must be encouraged to go fast. He should be helped to develop an attitude favourable to reading at the rate that his comprehension and the nature of materials allow. He should rather try to become unfavourably disposed to needlessly slow reading.

There are two main views about the best method of procedure for improving the rate of reading. One of them is based on the principle of giving direct practice for the improvement of eye movements. The other relies on providing practice on easy reading material with a high degree of motivation. Direct practice for the improvement of eye movements can easily be given through the mechanical devices meant for rate improvement.

The importance of perceptual training in rapid reading programmes cannot be underestimated. The reader with a narrow span of recognition, a slow rate of word recognition or a tendency to regress too often will remain a slow reader until these habits are corrected. Moreover, few people read to capacity, and the development of reading speed depends in substantial part upon the sharpening of the perceptual habits.

Mechanical Devices

Metronoscope, Tachistoscope, AVR Eye-Span Trainer, Controlled Reader, SRA Reading Accelerator, ATR Reading Rateometer, Excel-O-Reader, EDL Skimmer and Films are some of the mechanical devices used for sharpening the eye movements and breaking the reader's accustomed habits of slow reading.

Metronoscope: It is a tripple-shutter, short-exposure instrument designed to control reading. The tripple-shutter feature is so arranged that the shutters open in sequence from left to right in a rhythmical pattern, causing readers to read in a left-to-right sequence followed by an accurate return sweep. Because the shutters close after a short exposure, regressive movements within the printed line are discouraged. The reading matter is printed on a long roll, which unwinds so that one line of print is behind the shutters at a time. By varying the speed at which the shutters open and close, it is possible to vary the rate of presentation from very slow to extremely fast, at any speed that is desired. Good results from the use of the metronoscope have been reported by many.

One of the difficulties with the metronoscope is that it assumes that good readers read at a uniform rate throughout a selection, and make exactly three fixations on each line.

Eye movement studies show, however, that good readers vary their rate somewhat during the reading of a selection, and that few if any of them consistently make three fixations to each line. Instead their rate and fixations continually change according to the material they read.[1]

Tachistoscope: A tachistoscope is an apparatus for measuring speed of vision. It is composed of a camera box without lenses or arrangement to accommodate a film. The shutter of the apparatus can be set for various speeds like a camera shutter. One looks into the apparatus and gets a hasty glance at letters or numbers or whatever is exhibited in the apparatus. Tachistoscope requires a person to see more accurately, more rapidly and more orderly. He also develops a better directional attack. Since the tachistoscope span is greater than the span in normal reading, one can ask: what are the effects of tachistoscopic training; and is there any value in increasing the tachistoscopic span!

"Seeing" can be improved, and tachistoscopic training is one of the better ways of doing this. It has been used in the Armed Services, in remedial reading, in orthoptics, in teaching spelling and arithmetic, in business education and even in physical education. In each instance the emphasis has been on the development of general accuracy in seeing and remembering.[2] As a result of tachistoscopic training the reader learns self-discipline, better habits of work and better eye-hand coordination while improving his focusing ability. Most training on this apparatus is at high speeds.

AVR Eye-Span Trainer: An eye-span trainer (model 10) is a simple and effective hand operated shutter for individual training in flash recognition of words, phrases, numbers and other training items. The tachistoscope-type training given by the eye-span trainer helps the reader to see more in a single eye pause, to perceive more accurately, and to increase the number of visual perception per unit of time. Eye-span training is often undertaken before or concurrently with rateometer practice.

Controlled Reader: Controlled reader presents materials in a left-to-right direction at a pre-determined rate. A moving slot travels across the screen in a left-to-right direction, covering and uncovering the materials as it moves along.

Controlled reading, then, refers to a form of training in which timed presentations of reading or other visual materials are employed to condition more efficient visual-functional and perceptual processes in reading. In essence, controlled reading provides a reading situation to which a student accommodates and in doing so he conditions himself in a manner that leads to more efficient oculo-motor and perceptual behaviour. The most popular and widespread application of the controlled reading technique is in the development of fluent and efficient silent reading.

Training on controlled reader improves perceptual accuracy and efficiency. The left-to-right and rapidly moving projection slot accelerates a student's reading and at the same time encourages the student to approach each line of print in more efficient and sequential manner. These changes are best understood by studying the training phenomenon that occurs in the case of a given student.

One high school boy, before training, read at 215 words per minute, averaged 105 fixations per 100 words (or employed an average span of .95 words per fixation), made 20 regressions per 100 words (regressing once every five words on the average), and paused during each fixation for .27 of a second on the average.

When reading Controlled Reader stories that contain six words per line, his tendency would be to make approximately six fixations per line (including a regression) and to continue to pause for his habitual .27 of a second each time that he stops his eyes. But when the controlled reader is set at 240 words per minute, slightly faster than his usual rate, certain predictable modifications occur.

The student first fixates on the beginning of the line of print that is exposed. During the fixation pause time he commences to identify, recognise, and process word impressions with a perceptual awareness that favours the print to the right of his fixation point as is typical of all readers reading English.[3, 4 and 5]

The projection slot, moving along the line of print at a faster than usual rate (240 wpm) soon obliterates the student's fixation point as the point on which he was fixating is covered up. Though the student continues to react to the print to the right of his fixation point, fixating on blankness encourages him to refixate to the right sooner than he would normally do.[6]

Because his duration of fixation (length of eye-pause) tends to be quite habitual, the moving slot will "catch" the student time and time again, each time decreasing the amount of time he is allowed to spend reacting to the print (at 240 words per minute, he will most probably spend only .25 of a second per fixation). Over a period of time reading at faster and faster projection rates, the student's duration of fixation will be appreciably reduced as he learns to react to and process words more rapidly.[7]

SRA Reading Accelerator: A reading pacing device known as 'SRA Reading Accelerator' helps the reader in improving his reading ability specifically, the reading accelerator provides a reading situation in which a moving shutter travels at a constant rate down a page of printed material. The shutter may be adjusted for different speeds, depending on the material being read and on the individual's ability to read at the beginning of the training period. The shutter moves smoothly, covering successive lines of print and challenging the reader to keep ahead as his eye movements progress across each line and down the page. This training situation creates an incentive for the development and improvement of good reading habits. It encourages good phrasing, effective movements, and increased span of perception. It stimulates interest and improves mental concentration by breaking habits of word-by-word reading, vocalising, and unnecessary eye-movement regressions. The following are the two limitations of the SRA Reading Accelerator:

(*a*) The breadth of the window of the accelerator is 4½". It means that the material cannot be read if the width of the printed line exceeds 4½". Thus it becomes a serious handicap for some reading materials. To overcome this limitation, reading materials have got to be specifically printed or cyclostyled within the size-limit 7½" x 4½".

(*b*) While reading, the shutter of the accelerator moves over the window through which material is read. Frequent use of the accelerator leaves scratches of the shutter over the window and these cannot be removed.

AVR Reading Rateometer: It is another variety of reading accelerator in which a T-bar moves down the page and the student learns to improve reading rate by learning to lengthen eye spans, avoid regressions, speed eye fixations.

Excel-O-Reader: The Excel-O-Reader is a simple pocket-sized plastic instrument which exposes a word or phrase for 1/25th, 1/50th or 1/100th of a second. It eventually makes the person to read and understand five-word phrases in 1/100th of a second.

EDL Skimmer: The only machine available today that is designed to develop the skimming skill is the EDL Skimmer. This machine is equipped with a bead of light that travels down the centrefold of the book at the rate of one and a half minute per page, or about eight hundred to one thousand words per minute. This informs the reader how rapidly he should proceed and keeps him perceptually alert. The device is useful also in developing scanning skills.

Films: Some films for improving the reading skill are also used. These films help the reader to consolidate his knowledge of the rapid reading techniques.

Machines Serve as a Moral Booster

Mechanical devices for improving reading rate have motivational value. These instruments serve as a moral booster for the reader. They may even increase comprehension achievement.

Persons working with mechanical devices repeatedly have noticed among students an increase in interest in reading and in a desire to improve their reading skills. For some of these a successful experience in a machine programme may develop a new attitude towards reading generally which may lead to an improved performance in a number of areas including rate of comprehension.[8]

Probably the chief value of instruments is twofold: they motivate attempts to read faster, and they show a person how fast he really can read when he is forced to proceed at a rapid rate.[9]

Quite possibly the machines have an initial advantage in that they provide novelty and interest in the improvement of reading. Unfortunately, after a time the novelty may wear off, and consequently, one of the chief reasons for success reported with instruments of this type may no longer operate.[10]

Thomas and Robinson[11] suggest:

Pacer training is motivational for most students and profitable for many as long as word recognition, vocabulary, and comprehension skills are already adequate. If not until such inhibiting factors are removed, forcing such training may be extremely harmful. In one reading laboratory a young man was in tears about his performance on the pacer. He was being forced to "read" faster and faster when he did not know the meanings of the words on the page.

When no blocks are present, remediation in the areas of rates of reading is rapid as compared with vocabulary and comprehension.

Evaluation of Devices

It is not the eyes but the mind that exerts most control over our reading rate. Unless we have some visual anomaly, our eye movements are reflections of our thought processes. We may fail to move our eyes "efficiently" because we do not know a word's meaning, because we stop briefly to reflect on the content, or because our lack of interest inhibits our concentration. No amount of machine training or eye-movement exercises will affect these causes of our slow rate of reading. If, on the other hand, we read slowly because we have developed a habitually slow rate, some of the machine exercises may help us improve by jolting us out of our usual habits.[12] A survey by Karlin of studies comparing machine-centred reading courses with those using more natural types of materials concluded that rate gains can be achieved by the use of machines. However, Karlin found that courses not using machines do as well or even surpass those using such devices.[13]

Arthur I. Gates[14] in a survey of "Eye Movements and Gadgets", suggests that somewhat fixed, regular patterns or eye movements encouraged by some mechanical devices may not be at all desirable. He found that many good readers demonstrate considerable irregularity and flexibility in their eye movements and, therefore, may be adversely affected by machine training. Gates further points out that another advantage often attributed to machines is their motivational value, either as novelties or because they appeal to special mechanical interests. But he could find no evidence of gains due to these or any other characteristics of the machines: "I, therefore, conclude that this survey failed to reveal any evidence of specific advantages in these mechanical exposure procedures for any kind of child, and that on the contrary, they seem more likely to mislead and interfere with the development of the most desirable reading patterns than do other types of instruction."

Dr Eloise Cason[15] undertook a study to determine the relative effects upon third-grade children of three programmes. One of these employed the metronoscope; another followed a programme which employed artificially phrased materials such as texts in which alternate phrases were underlined, separated by a blank space, or printed in a different colour; and the third was one in which the pupils engaged exclusively in free library reading. In commenting on this study, her sponsor, Arthur I. Gates, reported:

> This is ... I believe, a growing tendency to recognise that a well-rounded, varied programme of normal reading activities nicely adjusted to individual needs is a more fruitful remedial or preventive procedure than any one of the more specialised artificial types of remedial devices or stunts ... For the reading disability we rarely need anything more than the best and richest normal programme applied with particular care and intelligence to the individual case. The remedial reading expert who is dependent upon a special kit of tricks, stunts, devices, and gadgets is rapidly being driven out of fashion by the brute force of careful study and experimentation.[16]

Cason[17] herself comments: "It is reasonable to assume that the burden of proof rests with those who favour the introduction of such mechanical or artificial methods into the classroom. The point to be demonstrated is the effectiveness of the methods in meeting particular needs. Effectiveness implies not only that good results are produced but also that they are secured in the simplest and most economical manner. The evidence presented in this study showed that, at the level studied and under the limitations of the experimental conditions, these procedures were ineffective in the sense that results commensurate with the effort were not obtained. The results, moreover, showed that the reading habits of certain children were disorganised by subjecting them to this type of procedure. This evidence is not an indictment of the use of such methods under all circumstances. It is entirely possible that such methods may produce improvement in selected individuals who do not respond to other methods of treatment, or help pupils older or younger than those studied."

The use of mechanical aids for controlling the rate of reading does not eliminate the need for an attack on the underlying cause of inappropriate rates of reading. The machines may discourage dawdling habits of reading, but in themselves they do not eliminate the chief causes of unsatisfactory rate of comprehension, such as lack of skill in methods of word recognition, lack of skill in selecting details, difficulty in organising what is read, failure to read material critically, and inability to locate information rapidly. In fact, "controlled reading" can even have a detrimental effect upon some of these factors. For example, the person whose chief reason for slow reading is a difficulty in recognising words may develop even poorer habits of word recognition because he is not given to apply sound means of word identification. Nor can the efficient reader employ the flexible habits of reading that are needed to get meaning quickly. When he comes to a word that he must analyse, he wants to stop for a longer pause. He may find it advisable to make regressive movements if he discovers that he has just finished reading a point that he should note carefully. He will want to vary his rate in accordance with his purpose in reading rather than follow the operation of mechanical shutters that compel him to read every line or part of a line in the same time as preceding ones.[18]

Nila Banton Smith[19] remarks:

"More scientific evidence is needed in regard to transfer of the results of instrument training to natural reading situations, and retention of the speed attained with such practice. If instruments are used, care should be taken to ensure that the speed achieved while reading with the use of the instruments is transferred to natural reading. After the use of an instrument the teacher should give some such directive as this: 'You have found out how fast you can read when the instrument is forcing you. Now, do the same thing without the instrument. Force your own eyes along over the next article and see if you can keep up to the instrument speed.' By far the larger portion of the practice should be done while reading material under natural conditions, otherwise the speed attained during instrument work may not carry over and remain.

"The instruments, of course, are limited in the types of skills in which they give practice. They do not provide help in developing word identification ability, critical evaluation of what is read, study skills of specific types, flexibility in the use of speed in reading different materials for different purposes, and so on. Their chief function is to increase speed with accompanying checks on meanings. Gains in meanings usually are not outstanding. In other words, instruments should not be looked upon as a cure-all."

Group training with accelerating devices like metronoscope, controlled readers and tachistoscopes is at far-point. This is not desirable for the readers with myopic vision and also for those who have difficulties with fusion because they are required to improve rate while they are handicapped visually. At far-point, the person can also "read" more words than in normal reading This clearly indicates that very little transfer occurs from these machines to normal book reading where one has to read from a very near-point. Reading accelerator has been used in many courses with great advantage.

Machine-Centred Versus Book-Centred Programmes

There is no denying the fact that training on mechanical devices is frequently accompanied by rate improvement. It is also generally true that rate gains have an adequate degree of permanency. Cole,[20] Read,[21] Cosper and Kephart,[22] Mullins and Mowry,[23] and Weber[24] have reported follow-up studies that indicated permanency in rate gains. In reviewing five such studies, Spache found that 51 to 84 per cent of the improvement in rate was reported to be retained six to twelve months after training.[25]

Ray[26] reviews fifteen studies dealing with retention of gain since 1950. Seven indicated a retention of gain in reading rate, while five reported a decline, and three reported additional gain beyond the rate attained on the post test.

In one carefully-executed investigation of 62 adults ranging in age from seventeen to fifty years, the initial rates per minute ranged from 111 words to 333 words. At the end of twenty hour-long periods of corrective exercises the average raters ranged from 311 words to 469 words. In an experiment with business executives 18 hours of directed practice resulted in increases in the average rate from 198 words to 351 words per minute.[27] A programme for Air Force Officers—reported that the average rate per minute increased from about 240 to about 600 words.[28]

Cosper and Kephart[29] report that 38 college students were given a reading programme consisting of about 28 to 30 hours of training of which about half was on an accelerator. The group tachistoscope was used from ten to fifteen minutes per session. In addition a film was shown once a week, and every two weeks a difficult essay was read. The reading rate of this group increased significantly more than that of a comparable control group of 28 students. Comprehension did not change significantly.

Jones[30] reports significant gains from a Reading and Study Skills programme combining machine and book-centred techniques. Before training, the 98 students had an average comprehension percentile on the Iowa Silent Reading Test of 45. By the end of the programme the average percentile rank had increased to 96. The number of words read per minute increased from 212 to 570. Eye-movement photographs showed that the fixation pause had decreased and the span of recognition had increased from 1.16 words to 2.38 words.

Andrews[31] reports a steady increase in reading speed using about fifty ten-minute practice sessions during a school year. The practice consisted of reading easy material as rapidly as possible for a minute and then counting the words read. The reading materials used were of a low level of difficulty. Andrews suggests that improvement was due to the heavy emphasis on rate. He writes: "I emphasise completely the aspect of speed in the early drills and encourage the students to ignore completely the aspect of understanding. I 'insist' from the second test on that all students read at least 350 words a minute 'whether you understand anything or not'!"

Lewis[32] using 27 college students, compared two methods for increasing speed. He found that mechanical devices combined with an emphasis on comprehension, meaning and the structure of the material read were more effective than mechanical devices alone.

Cardwell[33] reports that an adult reading programme had significant success without using any machines. The average words per minute before the programme began were 297; after the 24 one-hour sessions, the average was 417 wpm. Comprehension increased by 18.75 per cent.

Bellows and Rush,[34] Johnson[35] and Thompson[36] also report gains in rate with book-centred approaches. Thompson's subjects were 438 US Air Force Officers. Using three groups—a book-group, a machine-group, and a control-group—he found that in the 21-hour course the book-centred approach resulted in speeds significantly higher than those attained by the machine approach.

Studies generally have found that a wide divergence exists between visual span as measured on the tachistoscope, and reading rate, and that an increase in visual span fails to produce significant gains in reading rate. It may well be that the reader uses a different span during motivated training than during normal reading. The mind, not the vision, generally seems to be the limiting factor. The evidence suggests that the more meaningful the material is to the individual, the wider will be his recognition span.

Taylor[37] observes that improvement in rate of reading can result from an increase in the amount of print that can be perceived and organised rapidly. He writes: "The primary value of short exposure training, therefore, in reading improvement, is to contribute to an increase in the size of the span of recognition, to increase the accuracy and precision of perception and to develop the reader's ability to organise perceived material more rapidly. One of the more important results from short exposure work, however, is the improvement in the overall personal organisation of the pupil. Usually pupils who have had such training tend to become more alert and observant.

Spache[38] suggests:

"It would seem more logical to implement the diagnosis of slow reading by proving simpler materials ... or to attack the problem more directly by trying to improve the poor vocabulary, word recognition, or word-analysis skills which may be directly causal."

He continues:

"More real and permanent growth in rate can be accomplished by teaching the student how and when to use rapid reading and by direct instruction in reading for ideas, scanning for single facts without actual reading, and skimming by reading only headings and topic and summary sentences. The student achieves flexibility in rate (which, after all, is the real aim of rate training) only by learning to vary his speed and reading techniques according to his purposes, the difficulty and style of the reading material, and his familiarity with the content of the reading matter."

In a later evaluation, Spache[39] points out that "While the training devices do seem to contribute to rate increases, in more carefully-controlled experiments this contribution is as often a reflection of teacher variance and perhaps motivation as it is an intrinsic result of the method." Studies by Freeburne[40] and Glock[41] both suggest that differences among teachers may be more significant than differences in method. And Schick[42] has emphasised training aids are teaching adjuncts, not teacher replacements.

Ten Commissioned Officers of the Indian Navy attended a rapid reading programme[43] of 2-week duration where timed reading practice was given on a wide variety of reading materials. Reading Accelerator was also used for boosting the reading speed. Along with discussion lectures some reading films were also shown. The pre-testing mean of the group was 212 words per minute whereas the post-testing mean came out to be 531 wpm. On an average, increase in reading speed of the group was 2½ times with 7.5 per cent increase in reading comprehension.

A combination of machine-centred and book-centred programme for the Senior Executives of State Bank of India[44] resulted in rate improvement with no loss in comprehension. Reading speed of the group before training was 209 words per minute and after a rapid reading course of 2-week duration, it rose to 383 words per minute.

A similar course of a shorter duration[45] also yielded significant gains in reading speed.

Poulton[46] surveyed reading courses in England, and found most of them based on the Harvard films. Additional reading passages, however, were prepared for British students. Reports indicated that "the average rate of reading normally started at 160 to 280 words per minute and ended at 340 to 500 words per minute, increasing by 40 to 130 per cent. There was more often a gain than a loss in comprehension ... Follow-ups on students show losses, but reading is still ahead of beginning rate."

Two sections of 48 students at Texas Christian University were given 7 weeks of speed training followed by 7 weeks of comprehension training. Two other sections of 48 students each were given the training in converse order. The subjective and objective results indicated that the first group, at the semester's end, read faster than the second group; and "there was no significant difference between groups on vocabulary, comprehension, or total test scores." (Speed training was given via tachistoscope, reading films, accelerator reading, and timed reading exercises; comprehension group discussed vocabulary, main ideas, author's purpose, study skills, concentration, and memory.) The experiment indicated that if poor comprehension is a result of slow speed, then speed might be taught first, but with care and not with younger groups.[47]

College freshmen were divided into groups—one group was taught with Harvard films, the second with experimental films which allowed two full lines of print to be seen, and the third with books. All materials were the same. All methods resulted in improved eye movements, as well as improved reading rate, according to Traxler High School Reading Test, Iowa Silent Reading Test, and the Blommers Rate of Comprehension Test no method was best, but some teachers were more effective.[48]

Berger[49] found that all four methods—tachistoscopic, controlled reader, controlled pacing, and paperback scanning—produced significant gains in rate, the paperback scanning method being significantly superior to the other methods. No significant change appeared in comprehension level. All but tachistoscopic method produced gains in flexibility. All gains were retained when checked eight weeks after the completion of training.

McBride[50] criticises current views on increasing rate of reading. He presents unorthodox views and methods, and also makes claims of over 100,000 words a minute.[51]

McBride expands further on a speed-reading programme where three books are read simultaneously.[52]

Laffitte[53] reports on 56 college freshmen divided into three groups. One group received skimming practice exclusively; the second group, rapid reading drill only; the third group, skimming and rapid reading practice. The second and third groups used tachistoscopic and pacing devices. Training lasted two months. All the three groups significantly increased their reading rate, with most of the gains for the three groups occurring during the first month of training.

A study by Maxwell and Muller[54] involved 120 students at the University of Maryland. Forty were given a handout containing specific suggestions for increasing reading rate, with instructions to practice for a week. A second group of 40 students "were given materials designed to motivate them to read faster by stressing the importance of rapid reading but without a description of specific techniques." The remaining 40 students served as a control group. "The experimental group given techniques and urged to practice showed significantly greater rate gains (33 per cent improvement) than either the group receiving motivational material (11 per cent improvement) or the controls (9 per cent improvement)."

Karlin[55] reports on 13 investigations involving machines and reading done during previous two decades. These were grouped at four levels: elementary secondary, college, and adult. The results revealed that of the 12 studies measuring natural reading against machine reading, 11 of "the groups that received training in the former either equalled or surpassed the machine groups in rate of reading." Karlin suggests that more money should be spent on materials rather than on machines.

Morgan's study[56] involved 159 students from three sections of a reading improvement programme at Oklahoma A & M College during the Spring semester, 1956. Three groups were formed: one receiving supplementary tachistoscopic training, the second receiving tachistoscopic and controlled reader training; and, the third spending an equivalent amount of time on reading practice and exercise work. The control group was from an introductory psychology class. Measuring instruments were the Nelson-Denny Reading Test and the Baker words per minute Exercise. Morgan concluded that, regarding reading rate all three groups were superior to the control group with the non-machine group being superior to both the control and other two experimental groups. Bearing in mind the limitations of the study,

Morgan further concludes that "time spent, in a reading improvement programme, on practice reading exercises and vocabulary drill is more profitable to the student than the same amount of time devoted to training with mechanical devices."

In a doctoral study completed in 1966 at Boston University, Duffy[57] found that an extra-curricular reading clinic consisting of little but paced reading may actually be detrimental to college students with weaknesses in basic skills.

Following an investigation of the relevant literature, Tinker[58] suggests that training with the tachistoscope is of questionable value in increasing reading rate, although he observes that such training may produce other desirable effects, such as improved visual discrimination, greater attention, and heightened motivation. He also questioned the value of controlled pacing devices, noting that they are "no more effective in increasing rate of reading than are less complicated but sound classroom procedures." Pointing out that these machines are often expensive, he said, "their use becomes a ritual and tends to over-emphasise the mechanical aspects of reading to the sacrifice of proper attention to the more important process of comprehension and thinking," and, he added, "there is usually little transfer to natural reading situations." Taylor[59], President of Educational Development Laboratories, has pointed out that these machines are intended as "aids to the teacher ... and not a complete approach."

Tinker[60] reviewed studies on the use of pacing devices and concluded: The improvement obtained by eye-movement training with or without elaborate apparatus, is no greater than that resulting from motivated reading alone ... The use of pacing devices too often tends toward over-emphasis on the mechanics of reading to the sacrifice of adequate attention to the more important processes of perception, apprehension, and assimilation. This mechanical training may result in a decrease in flexibility and adaptability of reading habits. The tachistoscope is without value for increasing speed of reading. The money spent on the tachistoscope and rate controller devices might be better used for books and other supplies.

A detailed analysis of studies led George D. Spache to similar conclusions.[61]

It would seem that programmes for improving the rate of reading can be just as satisfactory without use of the elaborate mechanical gadgets. This assumes careful selection of materials, a properly organised programme, and competent instruction. If the teacher can provide the incentive which will motivate the pupil—"and most can"—machines or other gadgets are not necessary to achieve satisfactory gains in speed of reading. That is, the use of machines does increase speed of reading but their use is not necessary to get equivalent gains.[62]

SUMMARY

Metronoscope, Tachistoscope, AVR Eye-Span Trainer, Controlled Reader, SRA Reading Accelerator, AVR Reading Rateometer, Excel-O-Reader, EDL Skimmer and Reading Films are some of the mechanical devices used for rate improvement programmes. Mechanical devices for improving reading rate have motivational value. These instruments serve as a moral booster for the reader. Unquestionably, the mechanical devices have been effective in improving reading rate in may cases. How permanent the improvement has been is a matter of conjecture. A survey by Karlin of studies comparing machine-centred reading courses with those using more natural types of materials concluded that rate gains can be achieved by the use of machines. However, Karlin found that courses not using machines do as well or even surpass those using such devices. Spache also concluded that programmes for improving the rate of reading can be just as satisfactory without use of the elaborate mechanical gadgets. This assumes careful selection of materials, a properly organised programme and competent instruction. It must be remembered that while training devices do seem to contribute to rate increases, in more carefully controlled experiments this contribution is often a reflection of teacher variance and perhaps motivation as it is an intrinsic result of the method. And also that training aids are teaching adjuncts, not teacher replacements.

REFERENCES

1. Sission, E. D. "Habits of Eye-Movement in Reading", *Journal of Educational Psychology,* 28, (1937) 437-450.
2. Taylor, Stanford E and Frackenphol, Helen. *Teacher's Guide*: *Tach X Flash X,* Educational Developmental Laboratories, Huntington, New York, 1960, p. 6.
3. Hebb, D. O. *The Organization of Behaviour,* Wiley, New York, 1949.
4. Mishkin, M and Forgays, D. G. "Word Recognition as a Function of Retinal Locus", *Journal and Experimental Psychology,* 43, (1952), 43-48.
5. Ohrbach, J. "Retinal Locus as a Factor in Recognition of Visually Perceived Words", *American Journal of Psychology,* 65, (1953), 555-562.
6. Taylor, Stanford E and Frackenpohl, Helen. *Controlled Reading,* Teacher's Guide, Educational Developmental Laboratories, A Division of McGraw-Hill Book Company, New York, 1970, pp. 17-18.
7. Taylor, Stanford E and Frankhenpohl, Helen. *Controlled Reading* ... op. cit.
8. Dechant, Emerald. *Reading Improvement in the Secondary School,* Prentice-Hall, Inc., Englewood Cliffs, New Jersey, 1973, p. 329.
9. Smith, Nila Banton. *Reading Instruction for Today's Children,* Prentice-Hall, Inc., Englewood Cliffs, New Jersey, 1963, pp. 376-377.
10. DeBoer, John J and Dallmann, Martha. *The Teaching of Reading,* Holt, Rinehart and Winston Inc., New York, 1960, p. 161.
11. Thomas, Ellen Lamar and Robinson, Alan H. *Improving Reading in Every Class,* Abridged Ed, Allyn and Bacon, Inc., Boston, 1972, p. 158.
12. Hafner, Lawrence E and Jolly, Hayden B. *Patterns of Teaching Reading in the Elementary School,* The Macmillan Company, New York, 1972, p. 177.
13. Karlin, Robert K. "Machines in Reading: A Review of Research", *The Clearinghouse,* 32, (1958), 349-352.
14. Gates, A. I. "Eye-Movements and Gadgets", A Paper Read at the Meeting of the American Educational Research Association, Atlantic City, N.J., 1954.
15. Cason, Eloise B. *Mechanical Methods for Increasing the Speed of Reading—An Experimental Study at the Third Grade Level,* Columbia Contributions to Education No. 878, Bureau of Publications, Teachers College, Columbia University: New York, 1943.
16. Gates, Arthur I. "Diagnosis and Remediation in Reading", *The Elementary English Review,* 19, (December 1942), 239-240.
17. Cason, Eloise B. *Mechanical Methods for Increasing the Speed of Reading*...op. cit.
18. DeBoer, John J and Dallmam, Martha. *The Teaching of Reading,* Revised ed., Holt, Rinehart and Winston, Inc., New York, 1964, pp. 177-178.
19. Smith, Nila Banton. *Reading Instruction for Today's Children* ... op. cit.
20. Cole, George K. J "Adult Reading Clinic", *Library Journal,* 82, (February 1957), 497-500.
21. Read, James C. "Some Effects of Short Term Training in Reading Under Conditions of Controlled Motivation", *Journal of Educational Psychology,* 47, (May 1956), 257-264.
22. Cosper, Russell and Kephart, Newell C. "Retention of Reading Skills", *Journal of Educational Research,* 49, (November 1955), 211-216.

23. Mullins, Cecil J and Mowry, H W. "How Long Does Reading Improvement Last?" *Personnel Journal,* 32, (April 1954), 416-417.
24. Weber, C. O. "The Acquisition of Retention of Reading Skills by Freshmen", *Journal of Educational Psychology,* 30, (September 1939), 453-460.
25. Spache, George D. "A Rationale for Mechanical Methods of Improving Reading", *Significant Elements in College and Adult Reading Improvement,* Seventh Yearbook of the National Reading Conference, Texas Christian University Press, Fort Worth, 1958, 115-132, 118.
26. Ray, Darrel D. "The Permanency of Gains Made in College Reading Improvement Programmes", in J. Allen Figurel., (Ed), *Improvement of Reading Through Classroom Practice,* 1964 Proceedings, 9, International Reading Association, Newark, Delaware, 1964, pp. 192-193.
27. Holmes, Jack A. "Gifted Adults can Learn to Read Faster", *California Journal of Educational Research,* (Mary 1953), 103-110.
28. Jackson, J. L. "A Progress Report on the Reading Laboratory at the Air Command and Staff School", *School and Society,* 78 (2011), (July 11, 1953).
29. Cosper, Russell and Kephart, Newell C. "Retention of Reading Skills".... op. cit.
30. Jones, Ernest A. "A Small College Reading Programme", *Techniques and Procedures in College and Adult Reading Programmes,* The Sixth Yearbook of the Southwest Reading Conference for Colleges and Universities, Texas Christian University Press, Fort Worth, 1957, 7-15.
31. Andrews, Joe W. "An Approach to Speed Reading", *English Journal,* 41, (September 1952), 355.
32. Lewis, Norman. "An Investigation into Comparable Results Obtained from two Methods of Investigation Reading Speed Among Adults", *College English,* 11, (December 1949), 152-156.
33. Cardwell, Irene. "Adult Reading Improvement Without Machines", *School and Society,* 82, (September 1955), 71-72.
34. Bellows, Carol S and Rush, Carl H. Jr. "Reading Abilities of Business Executives", *Journal of Applied Psychology,* 36, (February 1952), 1-4.
35. Johnson, Janet Bassett. "Reading Clinic for Adults", *Clearing House,* 24, (December 1949), 195-198.
36. Thompson, Warren Craig. "A Book-Centred Course Versus a Machine-Centred Course in Adult Reading Improvement", *Journal of Educational Research,* 49, (February 1956), 437-445.
37. Taylor, Earl A. "The Spans: Perception, Apprehension, and Recognition", *American Journal of Opthalmology,* 44, (October 1957), 503.
38. Spache, George D. "Integrating Diagnosis with Remediation in Reading", *The Elementary School Journal,* 56, (September 1955), 22.
39. Spache, George D. *Reading Instruction for Today's Children,* op. cit.
40. Freeburne, Cecil Max. "The Influence of Training in Perceptual Span and Perceptual Speed Upon Reading Ability", *Journal of Educational Psychology,* 40, (February 1949), 321-352.
41. Glock, Marvin L. "The Effect Upon Eye-Movements and Reading Rate at the College Level of Three Methods of Training", *Journal of Educational Psychology,* 40, (February 1949), 93-106.

42. Schick, George B. "New Frontiers in Teaching Reading to College Groups", *New Frontiers in Reading,* Conference Proceedings, International Reading Association, Scholastic Magazines, New York, 1960, 44-49.

43. Report of the Rapid Reading Course for the Commissioned Officers of the Indian Navy held at the Central Institute of Indian Languages, Mysore from 7 to 21 April, 1975.

44. Report of the Rapid Reading Course for the Senior Executives of the State Bank of India conducted by the Central Institute of Indian Languages, Mysore at State Bank Staff College, Hyderabad from 15 to 29 December, 1975.

45. Report of the Second Rapid Reading Course for the Senior Executives of the State Bank of India conducted by the Central Institute of Indian Languages, Mysore at State Bank Staff College, Hyderabad from 17 to 22 May, 1976.

46. Poulton, E. C. "British Courses for Adults on Effective Reading", *British Journal of Educational Psychology,* 31, (1961), 128-137.

47. Rankin, Earl F. Jr. "Sequential Emphasis Upon Speed and Comprehension in a College Reading Improvement Programme", *Journal of Development Reading,* 7, (Autumn 1963), 46-54.

48. Glock, Marvin L. The Effect upon age movements and Reading Rate at College Level, op. cit.

49. Berger, Allen. "Effectiveness of Four Methods of Increasing Reading Rate, Comprehension, and Flexibility", in J. Allen Figurel (Ed.), *Forging Ahead in Reading,* 1967, Proceedings Vol. 12 Part 1, International Reading Association, Newark, Delaware, 1968, pp. 588-596. (Doctoral dissertations, Syracuse University, 1966).

50. McBride, Vearl G. "Worthwhile Reading: A Time for Action!" *North Carolina Education,* 15, (January 1967), 34.

51. McBride, Vearl G. "Adding Speed as You Read", *Florida Education,* 42, (September 1964), 14-15.

52. McBride, Vearl G. "Rapid Reading—Dr. McBride Responds", *Florida Education,* 42, (November 1964).

53. Laffitte, Rondeau G. Jr. "Analysis of Increased Rate of Reading of College Students", *Journal of Development Reading,* 7, (Spring 1964), 165-174.

54. Maxwell, Martha J and Mueller, Arthur C. "Relative Effectiveness of Techniques and Placebo Conditions in Changing Reading Rates", *Journal of Reading,* 11, (December 1967), 184-191.

55. Karlin, Robert K. "Machines in Reading: A Review of Research"... op. cit.

56. Morgan, Robert M. "The Relative Effectiveness of Mechanical and Non-Mechanical Methods in a Reading Improvement Programme", Master's Thesis, Oklahoma Agricultural and Mechanical College, Stillwater, Oklahoma, 1956.

57. Duffy, Thomas Francis. "A Small College Reading Programme: Required Paced Reading Followed by a Voluntary Clinic With Self-Instruction Through Programme Materials", Doctoral Dissertation, Boston University, School of Education, 1966.

58. Tinker, Miles A. "Uses and Limitations of Speed of Reading Programmes in Schools", *Speed Reading: Practices and Procedures,* 10, (March 1962), University of Delaware, Newark Delaware, 9-18.

59. Taylor, Stanford E. "Reading Instrument Usage", *Reading Teacher,* 15, (May 1962), 449-454.

60. Tinker, Miles A. "Devices to Improve Speed of Reading", *The Reading Teacher*, 20, (1967), 605-609.

61. Spache, George D. "Rate of Reading—The Machine Approach", *Toward Better Reading*, Garrard Publishing Company, Champaign, Illinois, 1963.

62. Tinker, Miles A and McCullough, Constance M. *Teaching Elementary Reading*, Fourth Edition, Prentice-Hall, Inc., Englewood Cliffs, New Jersey, 1975, p. 263.

LET US HAVE A DIALOGUE

(Here is an imaginary conversation between the reader and the book.)

Reader. Now-a-days people seem to be too much concerned about 'Reading'. It is the most discussed subject in all kinds of gatherings where the discussion revolves round the point as to how reading is done. Could you tell us what happens when a person reads?

Book. The reader perceives the words, comprehends their meanings, reacts to them and assimilates them. He also applies the assimilated reading materials in different situations according to the purpose at hand. Perceiving the words is just a mechanical process but comprehension involves mental processes. Since reading is always an intentional behaviour, different levels of reading work at different occasions according to the particular intention of the reader.

Reader. I am sorry—I can't just imagine the way in which reading as intentional behaviour is explained by you. Do you mean a person with bad intention gets negative feelings out of his reading and that a person reading with good intention gets something positive. I do not think reading is always intentional. Many times I myself turn the pages of a book without any intention. What have you to say here?

Book. Well, in the present context when I talk of reading as intentional behaviour, I do not think in terms of the intention being either good or bad. By intentional behaviour I only mean a purposeful behaviour. If your purpose is to get the literal level meaning of the reading material, you can go very fast about it but on the other hand if you are interested in getting the implied or even critical level comprehension, you will pause for a while in-between and ponder over the whole situation. Similarly, if your intention is to go through the whole paper in just five minutes, you will follow a fantastic speed and skim through the whole paper. When you say that sometimes you keep turning the pages without any intention, you may not be quite aware of the intention but the intention is all the same very much there. Sometimes you are turning the pages just to kill time particularly when you are waiting for somebody, waiting for a train or waiting in a clinic for your turn. In fact it is your intention, may be, at the conscious or unconscious level that orders your eyes to act in the reading process.

Reader. What do you have in mind when you use the term 'Reading process?'

Book. Reading in any language involves the interpretation of graphic shapes that stand for spoken words. Psychological and physiological processes involved in the reading process are highly complex. It is in a way a twofold process. It is a sensory and a mental process. As a sensory process it involves identification of the printed symbols with the help of eye movements and as a mental process, it takes help from the mind.

Reader. How does the eye behave during the reading process?

Book. Reading is the greatest task that the human eye can perform. Research evidence shows that the eyes do not move continuously along the printed symbols of a line. They move with short and quick jerky movements and stops, followed by a return sweep each time one completes reading a line. Here, you can compare the work of the eyes with that of the legs when we are busy in rope skipping. It is a go-stop—go-stop task of the eye.

Reader. What are eye movements?

Book. As the term indicates, these are the movements of the eyes in the reading process. The technical terms for eye movements are fixation pauses, interfixation movements, regressive movements, return sweeps, and refixations. The fixations are the pauses during which the eyes view the print, the interfixation movement is the movement from one fixation to the next. Regressions are the movements backward along the line of print to correct any misreading.

Reader. What happens during these eye jerks or interfixation movements in terms of reading?

Book. Nothing, because the eyes catch clear images only when they pause, never when in motion. When the eye moves from one fixation to another, clear vision of the print is not possible.

Reader. How much time does it take for the eye to go from one fixation to another?

Book. The interfixation movements are always of a very short duration, lasting a little over one-hundredth of a second on the average (10 to 23 milliseconds each) in the case of the good reader. This duration becomes comparatively longer in case of a poor reader.

Reader. When a person reads, what role do these fixation pauses have to play? What is their average duration, and how much is seen during these pauses when the eyes glance over the printed symbols?

Book. Reading requires seeing. Eyes are not able to see when they are moving. In order to see, they have to stop moving and fixate at certain point. If the eye does not fixate at all, we are not able to read so the eye fixations have a very important role to play in the reading act. For the mature reader, these fixation pauses have a duration of 250 milliseconds on the average. A good reader takes one-fifth of a second during each fixation pause; the poor reader requires twice or even thrice as long.

Of course the duration of these fixations may be shorter in easier and more familiar material.

Perhaps you would know that the amount of print which the eye is able to see during one fixation is called 'span of recognition' or 'span of perception'. This perception span averages 13 to 14 letter spaces for good readers, 6 spaces for poor readers. The wider the span of perception the lesser the number of fixation in each line, and the lesser the number of fixations, the greater the reading speed.

As you glance at the printed lines, you are able to see some elements clearly, others vaguely in the marginal vision. Each successive fixation brings new material into clear vision which before was seen only vaguely. (Incidentally, in the human eye the field of vision is the area the eyes can view distinctly while they are fixed upon some given point. The field of clearest vision is the fovea in the centre of the eye. Surrounding the fovea is the macula, the area of less distinct vision. The field of distinct vision has no clear-cut boundary, but shades off gradually on both sides).

Now, the size of the perception span can be obtained by dividing the length of the average line in the text read by the average number of pauses in a line. No doubt wider span of recognition helps in faster reading yet there is a physiological perceptual limit beyond which one is not able to go.

Reader. What effect does the nature of the content have on the length of 'span of recognition'?

Book. I don't think there is any. Even though the reading material is of easy and interesting nature for the individual, our eyes cannot cross the physiological perceptual limit. Of course the number of fixation pauses in a line depends to some extent on the length of the line, and the amount of print in any line varies with the size of type.

Reader. Which is more important, the mechanics of the eye movements or the mental process of interpreting the symbols in print?

Book. Neither, since the latter is always dependent on the former. For example, if the eye movements are quite good, there is no problem of vision, eyes are alert but the message even if registered in the brain does not have any response, reading cannot take place. Similarly if the mind is working all right and is always ready to receive the messages but message gaining organs (say eyes in this case) are not able to send the message, reading cannot take place, so I suppose both the eye movements and the mental process of interpreting, are important.

Reader. How can we change our slow reading habits?

Book. Our present reading habits are the result of our early habits which we have been practising over a period of years. These habits which are so much fixed and practised for many years, are hard to break. In the process of substituting new habits for the old ones, we may encounter many feelings of insecurity. Therefore, if we are really interested in giving up old habits in favour of the new ones, we have to strive hard for breaking our accustomed tempo. This task may at first appear difficult but it is quite within your easy reach. The only thing you have to cultivate is the willingness to work, a hardworking attitude and a competitive spirit within yourself. Since reading is a skill, it responds readily to practice. However, the practice should be continuous and systematic to begin with.

Reader. What do we mean by systematic reading practice? Do you mean more and more regular reading practice will improve our reading speed?

Book. By systematic practice, I mean a regular and systematised reading practice which is totally free of crutches. Efficient reading habits are a must for every one of us. If as an adult, you are using inefficient reading habits, it is obvious that even more and more reading practice will not automatically result in improved reading skills. The more you read, the more you reinforce whatever inefficient reading habits you may already have. This will be true unless you are ready to make some systematic effort to eliminate your present habits which stand between you and efficient reading. You must practise new habits and this practice will have to be a systematic one. Reading ability can be improved through the systematic practice of more effective reading habits. I hope I am quite clear.

Reader. It is clear but ... I could not follow about the crutches, inefficient reading habits and also what exactly do you mean by effective reading habits?

Book. As the word suggests, 'crutches' give support in reading. Some common type of crutches are vocalisation, sub-vocalisation, finger pointing and head movement. These crutches are not considered bad when we as children start learning reading but once the mechanics of reading have been mastered and reading speed is to be taken into account, these crutches hinder the reading speed. Some readers are so much used to oral reading that they find it very difficult to read silently. As a result, when they have to read silently they keep moving their lips as if they were reading orally to themselves. This slows down their reading speed because speech normally occurs at about 125 or 150 words per minute.

A more common and more serious reading problem is sub-vocalisation which occurs when a reader says each word to himself as he reads "internally". He does not actually say the words aloud (this would be "vocalisation"): but even though he is "reading to himself" all the muscles involved in speech come into play as he sub-vocalises quietly. The greater the amount of sub-vocalisation, the lower the speed of reading. You should make an effort to read faster and to concentrate on the author's ideas and not to go through the motions of having an "internal radio announcer" reading each word.

Again, finger pointing is another crutch which hinders the reading speed because the fingers cannot move as fast as the eyes can move. Similarly, head movements do not help in faster reading, rather they create reading fatigue. There is a general misunderstanding among the people that it improves their speed or comprehension to turn their head from one side to another while reading a book. This is wrong. The eye muscles are quite capable of doing the job of aiming the fovea at the print. The neck muscles accomplish nothing in the reading process.

You will have thus realised that reading ability is made up of a large number of skills. The absence of some of these skills, is frequently noted among immature and inexperienced readers. On the other hand there are some inefficient reading habits which can be observed even among adults. These are: Lack of flexibility in reading rate, word by word reading, word analysis, inefficient use of context clues, lack of phrasing, etc. Efficient reading habits involve sharpening of visual perception as it relates to word perception, reading in thought units and minimising "sub-vocalisation" or "saying" the words mentally when reading silently.

Reader. How fast should one read?

Book. One cannot and should not have a set reading speed for every type of reading task. An efficient reader always makes use of several reading speeds. Even in one reading task at one sitting an efficient reader goes at speeds like 1000 to 1200 and 200 to 300 words per minute. He may sometimes skim over some parts of the reading material at the rate of more than 3000 words per minute. Skimming and scanning always demand fantastic speeds. Edward Fry in his book '*Reading Instruction for Classroom and Clinic*' (McGraw-Hill Book Company, New York, 1972, p. 429) gives a comparative view of different reading speeds of poor and good readers which may be of interest to you. You can refer to it right here.

Speed		Poor reader	Good reader
Slow	Study reading speed is used when material is difficult and/or high comprehension is desired.	100-200 w.p.m. 80-90% comp.	200-300 w.p.m. 80-90% comp.
Average	Average reading speed is used for everyday reading of magazines, newspapers and easier textbooks.	150-250 w.p.m. 70% comp.	300-600 w.p.m. 70% comp.
Fast	Skimming is used when the highest rate is desired. Comprehension is intentionally lower.	Cannot skim	1000+ w.p.m.

Reader. I quite agree with you on skimming and scanning speeds but in case of straight reading (which goes horizontally from left to right) there is I believe a physiological limit beyond which a person cannot go. Let us assume that the reader can recognise and comprehend the maximum span of three words per fixation, and that there are no regressions, the line of 10 words is read in .66 of a second, or at a rate of approximately 15 words per second, i.e., 900 words per minute. Any speed greater than this is not possible. To my mind the speeds of 1000 and 1200 are impossible, if not fantastic!

Book. I quite appreciate the calculations presented by you but an efficient reader while making use of contextual constraints is able to go faster because he need not necessarily see each and every word.

Reader. How does rapid reading help when one is required to read critically or perform study reading?

Book. A rapid reader is always a smart reader. He takes reading as an active process. He refers to many sources with wind-like speeds in a limited time and is able to give his own judgement while reading critically. On the basis of more and more reading (which at one stage he can do at faster speed) he can differentiate between fact and opinion. A critical reader makes use of several speeds. Study reading also demands fast reading habits. Skimming is used while previewing and reviewing.

Reader. Even so, I have one doubt. Don't you think faster reading lowers reading comprehension? I personally feel that slow readers are better comprehenders. Could you please enlighten me on this point?

Book. Yes, you are right. Apparently one may feel that a fast reader tends to be inaccurate and poor in comprehension while a slow reader is accurate and comprehends better. But research gives a contrary opinion. Fast readers are better comprehenders. At this point one should always bear in mind—even a fast reader does not necessarily read everything fast. Faster reading speeds in subjects like science and mathematics may lead to disastrous results. In general, faster reading does not lower comprehension and fast readers are better comprehenders.

Reader. If fast readers comprehend better than slow readers, should slow readers then try to increase their reading speed in order to improve their comprehension?

Book. No. Not at all. If they do so, they will become more careless while rushing through their reading materials. If the slowness is due to certain bad habits, slow readers can benefit permanently from attempts to achieve a faster rate by eliminating the bad habits. If slow reading speed is due to poor comprehension, the readers should be helped in improving their reading comprehension first. In this case, understanding and not speed should be the primary aim.

Reader. Will reading improvement training in one language help one to improve in another language?

Book. Why not? Reading ability is a general power. It is not confined to one language. Reading improvement in one language is automatically transferred to another language provided the languages in question are used by the reader with equal ease.

Reader. Can I improve my reading speed? When should I start?

Book. Your eyes function very much like a camera. They take a picture of the words you are reading and flash them to your brain. Your brain instantly interprets the meaning of the words. If you teach your eyes to take larger pictures at each stop, they wouldn't have to stop very often. Larger pictures mean more words flashed to the brain at each stop and your brain has the capacity to interpret phrases or even whole sentences in a flash.

In short, almost everyone who is able to read can learn to read better. You too can improve your reading rate. Why not start right now? Try to grasp the science of reading and start practising on the suggested guidelines. Remember that faster reading is a big business where investment is meagre, gains are plenty. Entertainment through reading is not at all costly but pleasures are lasting. Rapid reading habits cost nothing but gives a lot. The miracle of better reading will take you a long way on the path of unlimited benefits. Rapid reading is a sure way to knowledge and knowledge is power reading — a power which makes you supreme. Increase your reading power and lead a better, fuller and richer life.

Reader. I would like to know from you whether rapid reading helps in better concentration?

Book. Nothing makes concentration so easy, so immediate, as the technique of sweeping through material purposefully looking for main ideas and broad concepts. If, through laziness, you read at a slower rate than the rate at which you are able to comprehend, there is a great temptation for your mind to wander. For example, the brightest pupils in a class are not always the best students. If the work is too easy for them, they become bored, they think of more interesting things, they daydream, they stop paying attention. This analogy explains why a slow reader picks up a book or magazine, goes through a few pages, and finding that his attention is wandering, puts it down and turns to something else. Fast aggressive reading sharpens your understanding and enjoyment, for, every distracting thought is pushed out of your mind. My advice to all those who want to learn to concentrate better will be something like this: "Get yourself in the right mental state to concentrate. Most concentration difficulties stem from the fact that the mind is not occupied. Question and anticipate to become an active reader."